Jennifer L. Castle · David F. Hendry

Modelling our Changing World

Jennifer L. Castle
Magdalen College
University of Oxford
Oxford, UK

David F. Hendry
Nuffield College
University of Oxford
Oxford, UK

https://doi.org/10.1007/978-3-030-21432-6

Preface

This short introduction to *Modelling our Changing World* focuses on the concepts, tools and techniques needed to successfully model time series data. The basic framework draws on Hendry and Nielsen (2007), summarized in Hendry and Nielsen (2010) and Hendry and Mizon (2016). It emphasizes the need for general models to account for the complexities of the modern world and the magnitudes of the many changes that have occurred historically. The combination of evolutionary and abrupt changes poses a major challenge for empirical modelling and hence for developing appropriate methods for selecting models. Fortunately, many of the key concepts can be explained using simple examples. Moreover, computer software for automatic model selection can be used to undertake the more complicated empirical modelling studies.

Modelling our Changing World is aimed at general academic readers interested in a wide range of disciplines. The book is applicable to many areas within the sciences and social sciences, and the examples discussed cover our recent work on climate, volcanoes and economics. All disciplines using time series data should find the book of valuc. Thc level minimizes technicalities in favour of visual and textual descriptions, and provides a set of primers to introduce core concepts in an intuitive way. Any more technical discussion with mathematics occurs in boxed material and can be skipped without missing the key ideas and intuition. Undergraduates on environmental and economics courses including some statistics and econometrics should find it a useful complement to standard textbooks.

The book commences with some 'Primers' to elucidate the key concepts, then considers evolutionary and abrupt changes, represented by trends and shifts in a number of time series. Sometimes, we can use trends and breaks to our advantage, but first we must be able to find them in the data being modelled to avoid an incorrect representation. Once a good empirical model of changing series has been built combining our best theoretical understanding and most powerful selection methods, there remains the hazardous task of trying to see what the future might hold. Our approach uses *OxMetrics* (see Doornik 2018b) and *PcGive* (Doornik and Hendry 2018) as that is the only software that implements all the tools and techniques needed in the book. The software is available for download from www.timberlake.co.uk/software/oxmetrics.html. Most recently, XLModeler is an Excel add-in that provides much of the functionality of *PcGive*: see Doornik et al. 2019. More advanced Monte Carlo simulations also require *Ox* (see Doornik 2018a). The accompanying online appendix includes all files required to enable a full replication of the empirical example in Chapter 6, including data, algebra, and batch files using *OxMetrics*.

The references provide plenty of further reading for interested readers. For readers looking to follow up with a more technical treatment we recommend Hendry and Doornik (2014) for model selection, Clements and Hendry (1998, 1999) for forecasting, and Hendry (1995) for a comprehensive treatment of econometric modelling with time series data.

Oxford, UK

Jennifer L. Castle
David F. Hendry

References

Clements, M. P., and Hendry, D. F. (1998). *Forecasting Economic Time Series*. Cambridge: Cambridge University Press.

Clements, M. P., and Hendry, D. F. (1999). *Forecasting Non-stationary Economic Time Series*. Cambridge, MA: MIT Press.

Doornik, J. A. (2018a). *Object-Oriented Matrix Programming Using Ox*, 8th Edition. London: Timberlake Consultants Press.

Doornik, J. A. (2018b). *OxMetrics: An Interface to Empirical Modelling*, 8th Edition. London: Timberlake Consultants Press.

Doornik, J. A., and Hendry, D. F. (2018). *Empirical Econometric Modelling Using PcGive: Volume I*, 8th Edition. London: Timberlake Consultants Press.

Doornik, J. A., Hendry, D. F., and Laurent, L. (2019). XLModeler 1. https://xlmodeler.com/.

Hendry, D. F. (1995). *Dynamic Econometrics*. Oxford: Oxford University Press.

Hendry, D. F., and Doornik, J. A. (2014). *Empirical Model Discovery and Theory Evaluation*. Cambridge, MA: MIT Press.

Hendry, D. F., and Mizon, G. E. (2016). Improving the teaching of econometrics. *Cogent Economics and Finance*. https://doi.org/10.1080/23322039.2016.1170096. http://www.tandfonline.com/eprint/7dRymBhRtIQF2xtbvPMC/full.

Hendry, D. F., and Nielsen, B. (2007). *Econometric Modeling: A Likelihood Approach*. Princeton: Princeton University Press.

Hendry, D. F., and Nielsen, B. (2010). A modern approach to teaching econometrics. *European Journal of Pure and Applied Mathematics*, **3**, 347–369. https://ejpam.com/index.php/ejpam/article/view/796.

Acknowledgements

The background research was originally supported in part by grants from the Economic and Social Research Council, and more recently by the Open Society Foundations, the Oxford Martin School, the Institute for New Economic Thinking, the Robertson Foundation, and Statistics Norway. We are grateful to them all for the essential funding they provided, and to Jurgen A. Doornik, Neil R. Ericsson, Vivien L. Hendry, Andrew B. Martinez, Grayham E. Mizon, John N.J. Muellbauer, Bent Nielsen, Felix Pretis and Angela Wenham for helpful discussions and suggestions.

The book was prepared in *OxEdit* and initially typeset in LATEX using *MikTex*. Graphical illustrations, numerical computations and Monte Carlo experiments were done using *Ox*, *OxMetrics* and *PcGive*. The present release is *OxMetrics* 8.01 (November 2018).

Oxford
January 2019

Jennifer L. Castle
David F. Hendry

Contents

About the Authors

Dr. Jennifer L. Castle is Tutorial Fellow in Economics at Magdalen College, Oxford University, and a Fellow at the Institute for New Economic Thinking in the Oxford Martin School.

She previously held a British Academy Postdoctoral Research Fellowship at Nuffield College, Oxford. She is a former director of the International Institute of Forecasters, and has contributed to the fields of Model Selection and Forecasting from both theoretical and practical approaches, publishing in leading journals and contributing to the development of several software packages.

Professor David F. Hendry, Kt is Director of the Program in Economic Modeling at the Institute for New Economic Thinking and co-director of Climate Econometrics at Nuffield College, Oxford University.

He was previously Professor of Econometrics, London School of Economics. He was knighted in 2009, and received a Lifetime Achievement Award from the Economic and Social Research Council in 2014. He is an Honorary Vice-President and a past President of the Royal Economic Society, a Fellow of the British Academy, the Royal Society of Edinburgh, the Econometric Society, the Academy of Social Sciences, the *Journal of Econometrics*, *Econometric Reviews*, International Association for Applied Econometrics and the International Institute of Forecasters. Sir David is a Foreign Honorary Member of the American Economic Association and American Academy of Arts and Sciences. He has been awarded eight Honorary Doctorates, is listed by the ISI as one of the world's 200 most cited economists, is a Thomson Reuters Citation Laureate, and has received the Guy Medal in Bronze from the Royal Statistical Society. He has published more than 200 papers and 25 books on econometric methods, theory, modelling, computing & history; numerical techniques; empirical economics; and forecasting, for which he was awarded the Isaac Kerstenetzky Scholarly Achievement Award in 2012.

List of Figures

1

Introduction

Abstract The evolution of life on Earth—a tale of both slow and abrupt changes over time—emphasizes that change is pervasive and ever present. Change affects all disciplines using observational data, especially time series of observations. When the dates of events matter, so data are not ahistorical, they are called non-stationary denoting that some key properties like their means and variances change over time. There are several sources of non-stationarity and they have different implications for modelling and forecasting. This Chapter introduces the structure of our book which will explore how to model such observational data on an ever-changing world.

Keywords Change · Observational data · Stationarity · Non-stationarity · Forecast failure

Earth has undergone many remarkable events in its 4.5 billion years, from early forms of life through the evolution and extermination of enormous numbers of species, to the present day diversity of life. It has witnessed movements of continents, impacts from outer space, massive volcanism, and experienced changing climates from tropical through ice ages, and recent changes due to anthropogenic interventions following the devel-

J. L. Castle and D. F. Hendry, *Modelling our Changing World*,
Palgrave Texts in Econometrics, https://doi.org/10.1007/978-3-030-21432-6_1

opment of homo sapiens, especially since the industrial revolution. The world is ever changing, both slowly over time and due to sudden shocks. This book explores how we can model observational data on such a world.

Many disciplines within the sciences and social sciences are confronted with data whose properties change over time. While at first sight, modelling volcanic eruptions, carbon dioxide emissions, sea levels, global temperatures, unemployment rates, wage inflation, or population growth seem to face very different problems, they share many commonalities. Measurements of such varied phenomena come in the form of time-series data. When observations on a given phenomenon, say CO_2 emissions, population growth or unemployment, come from a process whose properties remain constant over time—for example, having the same mean (average value) and variance (movements around that mean) at all points in time—they are said to be *stationary*. This is a technical use of that word, and does not entail 'unmoving' as in a traffic jam. Rather, such time series look essentially the same over different time intervals: indeed, a stationary time series is ahistoric in that the precise dates of observations should not matter greatly. However, almost all social, political, economic and environmental systems are non-stationary, with means, variances and other features, such as correlations between variables, changing over time. In the real world, whether an event under consideration happened in 1914, 1929, 1945 or 2008 usually matters, a clear sign that the data are *non-stationary*.

Much of economic analysis concerns equilibrium states although we all know that economies are buffeted by many more forces than those contained in such analyses. Sudden political changes, financial and oil crises, evolution of social mores, technological advances, wars and natural catastrophes all impinge on economic outcomes, yet are rarely part of theoretical economic analyses. Moreover, the intermittent but all too frequent occurrence of such events reveals that disequilibrium is the more natural state of economies. Indeed, forecast failures—where forecasts go badly wrong relative to their expected accuracy—reveal that such non-stationarities do happen, and have adverse effects both on economies and on the verisimilitude of empirical economic models. Castle et al. (2019) provide an introduction to forecasting models and methods and the properties of the resulting forecasts, explaining why forecasting mishaps are so common.

To set the scene, the book begins with a series of primers on non-stationary time-series data and their implications for empirical model selection. Two different sources of non-stationarity are delineated, the first coming from evolutionary changes and the second from abrupt, often unanticipated, shifts. Failing to account for either can produce misleading inferences, leading to models that do not adequately characterise the available evidence. We then go on to explore how features of non-stationary time-series data can be modelled, utilising both well-established and recent innovative techniques. Some of the proposed new techniques may surprise many readers. The solution is to include more variables than you have observations for, which is important to capture the ever changing nature of the data. Nevertheless, both theoretical analyses and computer simulations confirm that the approach is not only viable, but has excellent properties.

Various examples from different disciplines demonstrate not only the difficulties of working with such data, but also some advantages. We will gain insights into a range of phenomena by carefully modelling change in its many forms. The examples considered include the underlying causes and consequences of climate change, macroeconomic performance, various social phenomena and even detecting the impacts of volcanic eruptions on temperatures. However, valuable insights from theoretical subject-matter analyses must also be retained in an efficient approach and again recent developments can facilitate doing so. Forecasting will inevitably be hazardous in an ever-changing world, but we consider some ways in which systematic failure can be partly mitigated.

The structure of the book is as follows. In Chapter 2, primers outline the key concepts of time series, non-stationarity, structural breaks and model selection. Chapter 3 explores some explanations for change and briefly reviews the history of time-series modelling. Chapter 4 looks at how to use the ever changing data to your advantage: non-stationarity in some form is invaluable for identifying causal relationships and conducting policy. Chapter 5 shows how various forms of break can be detected and hence modelled. Chapter 6 examines an empirical example of combining theory and data to improve inference. Chapter 7 looks at forecasting non-stationary time series, with hints on how to handle structural breaks over the forecast horizon, and finally Chapter 8 concludes.

Reference

Castle, J. L., Clements, M. P., and Hendry, D. F. (2019). *Forecasting: An Essential Introduction.* New Haven, CT: Yale University Press.

2

Key Concepts: A Series of Primers

Abstract This chapter provides four primers. The first considers what a time series is and notes some of the major properties that time series might exhibit. The second extends that to distinguish stationary from non-stationary time series, where the latter are the prevalent form, and indeed provide the rationale for this book. The third describes a specific form of non-stationarity due to structural breaks, where the 'location' of a time series shifts abruptly. The fourth briefly introduces methods for selecting empirical models of non-stationary time series. Each primer notes at the start what key aspects will be addressed.

Keywords Time series · Persistence · Non-stationarity · Nonsense relations · Structural breaks · Location shifts · Model selection · Congruence · Encompassing

J. L. Castle and D. F. Hendry, *Modelling our Changing World*,
Palgrave Texts in Econometrics, https://doi.org/10.1007/978-3-030-21432-6_2

2.1 Time Series Data

What is a time series and what are its properties?

A time series orders observations
Time series can be measured at different frequencies
Time series exhibit different patterns of 'persistence'
Historical time can matter

A Time Series Orders Observations

A time series is any set of observations ordered by the passing of time. Table 2.1 shows an example. Each year, a different value arises. There are millions of recorded time series, in most social sciences like economics and politics, environmental sciences like climatology, and earth sciences like volcanology among other disciplines.

The most important property of a time series is the *ordering* of observations by 'time's arrow': the value in 2014 happened before that in 2015. We live in a world where we seem unable to go back into the past, to undo a car crash, or a bad investment decision, notwithstanding science-fiction stories of 'time-travellers'. That attribute will be crucial, as time-series analysis seeks to explain the present by the past, and forecast the future from the present. That last activity is needed as it also seems impossible to go into the future and return with knowledge of what happens there.

Time Series Occur at Different Frequencies

A second important feature is the *frequency* at which a time series is recorded, from nano-seconds in laser experiments, every second for electricity usage, through days for rainfall, weeks, months, quarters, years, decades and centuries to millenia in paleo-climate measures. It is relatively easy to combine higher frequencies to lower, as in adding up the economic

Table 2.1 A short annual time series

Date	2012	2013	2014	2015	2016	2017
Value	4	6	5	9	7	3

output of a country every quarter to produce an annual time series. An issue of concern to time-series analysts is whether important information is lost by such temporal aggregation. Using a somewhat stretched example, a quarterly time series that went 2, 5, 9, 4 then 3, 4, 8, 5 and so on, reveals marked changes with a pattern where the second 'half' is much larger than the 'first', whereas the annual series is always just a rather uninformative 20. The converse of creating a higher-frequency series from a lower is obviously more problematic unless there are one or more closely related variables measured at the higher frequency to draw on. For example, monthly measures of retail sales may help in creating a monthly series of total consumers' expenditure from its quarterly time series. In July 2018, the United Kingdom Office for National Statistics started producing monthly aggregate time series, using electronic information that has recently become available to it.

Time Series Exhibit Patterns of 'Persistence'

A third feature concerns whether or not a time series, whatever its frequency, exhibits *persistent patterns.* For example, are high values followed by lower, or are successive values closely related, so one sunny day is most likely to be succeeded by another? Monthly temperatures in Europe have a distinct seasonal pattern, whereas annual averages are less closely related with a slow upward trend over the past century.

Figure 2.1 illustrates two very different time series. The top panel records the annual unemployment rate in the United Kingdom from 1860–2017. The vertical axis records the rate (e.g., 0.15 is 15%), and the horizontal axis reports the time. As can be seen (we call this ocular econometrics), when unemployment is high, say above the long-run mean of 5% as from 1922–1939, it is more likely to be high in the next year, and similarly when it is low, as from 1945–1975, it tends to stay low. By way of contrast, the lower panel plots some computer generated random numbers between −2 and +2, where no persistence can be seen.

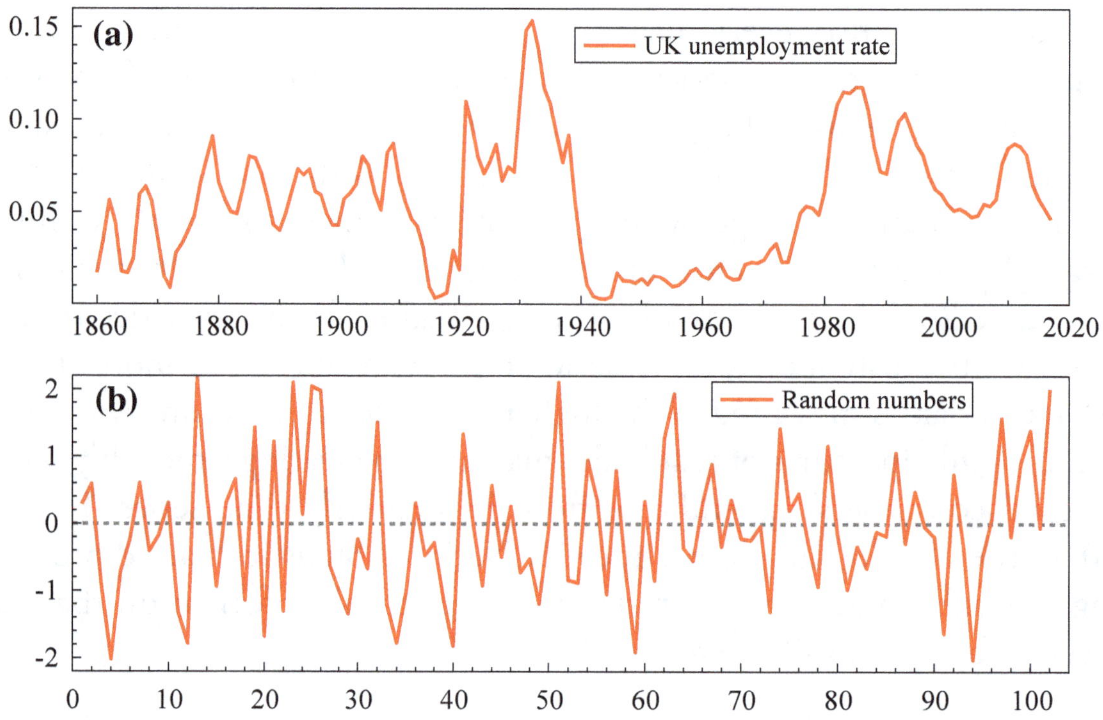

Fig. 2.1 Panel **(a)** UK annual unemployment rate, 1860–2017; **(b)** a sequence of random numbers

Many economic time series are very persistent, so correlations between values of the same variable many year's apart can often be remarkably high. Even for the unemployment series in Fig. 2.1(a), there is considerable persistence, which can be measured by the correlations between values increasingly far apart. Figure 2.2(a) plots the correlations between values r-years' apart for the UK unemployment rate, so the first vertical bar is the correlation between unemployment in the current year and that one year earlier, and so on going back 20 years. The dashed lines show an interval within which the correlations are not significantly different from zero. Note that sufficiently far apart correlations are negative, reflecting the 'long swings' between high and low unemployment visible in Fig. 2.1(a). Figure 2.2(b) again shows the contrast with the correlations between successively far apart random numbers, where all the bars lie in the interval shown by the dashed lines.

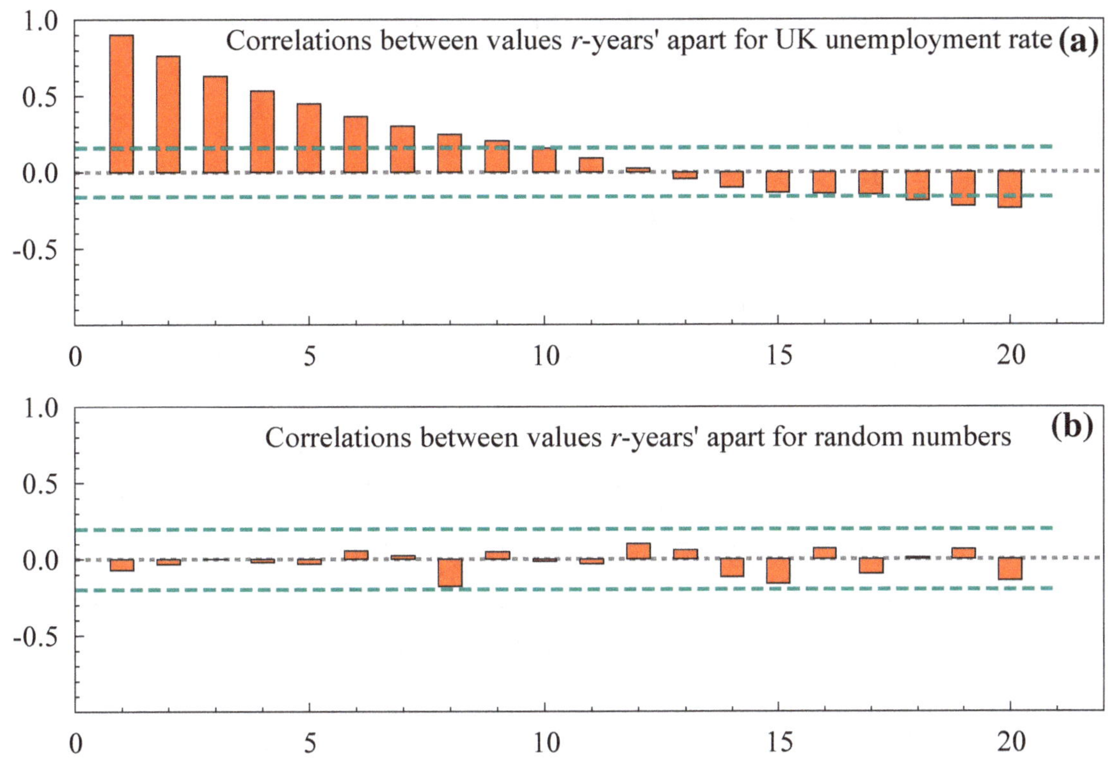

Fig. 2.2 Correlations between successively futher apart observations: (**a**) UK unemployment rates; (**b**) random numbers

Historical Time can Matter

Historical time is often an important attribute of a time series, so it matters that an event occurred in 1939 (say) rather than 1956. This leads to our second primer concerned with a very fundamental property of all time series: does it 'look essentially the same at different times', or does it evolve? Examples of relatively progressive evolution include technology, medicine, and longevity, where the average age of death in the western world has increased at about a weekend every week since around 1860. But major abrupt and often unexpected shifts can also occur, as with financial crises, earthquakes, volcanic eruptions or a sudden slow down in improving longevity as seen recently in the USA.

2.2 Stationarity and Non-stationarity

What is a non-stationary time series?

A time series is not stationary if historical time matters
Sources of non-stationarity
Historical review of understanding non-stationarity

A Time Series is Not Stationary if Historical Time Matters

We all know what it is like to be stationary when we would rather be moving: sometimes stuck in traffic jams, or still waiting at an airport long after the scheduled departure time of our flight. A feature of such unfortunate situations is that the setting 'looks the same at different times': we see the same trees beside our car until we start to move again, or the same chairs in the airport lounge. The word stationary is also used in a more technical sense in statistical analyses of time series: a stationary process is one where its mean and variance stay the same over time. Our solar system appears to be almost stationary, looking essentially the same over our lives (though perhaps not over very long time spans).

A time series is stationary when its first two moments, namely the mean and variance, are finite and constant over time.[1] In a stationary process, the influence of past shocks must die out, because if they cumulated, the variance could not be constant. Since past shocks do not accumulate (or integrate), such a stationary time series is said to be integrated of order zero, denoted $\mathsf{I}(0)$.[2] Observations on the process will center around the mean, with a spread determined by the magnitude of its constant variance. Consequently, any sample of a stationary process will 'look like' any other, making it *ahistorical*. The series of random numbers in Fig. 2.1(b) is an example. If an economy were stationary, we would not need to know the

---

[1]More precisely, this is weak stationarity, and occurs when for all values of t (denoted $\forall t$) the expected value $\mathsf{E}[\cdot]$ of a random variable y_t satisfies $\mathsf{E}[y_t] = \mu$, the variance, $\mathsf{E}[(y_t - \mu)^2] = \sigma^2$, and the covariances $\mathsf{E}[(y_t - \mu)(y_{t-s} - \mu)] = \gamma(s)\ \forall s$, where μ, σ^2, and $\gamma(s)$ are finite and independent of t and $\gamma(s) \to 0$ quite quickly as s grows.

[2]When the moments depend on the initial conditions of the process, stationarity holds only asymptotically (see e.g., Spanos 1986), but we ignore that complication here.

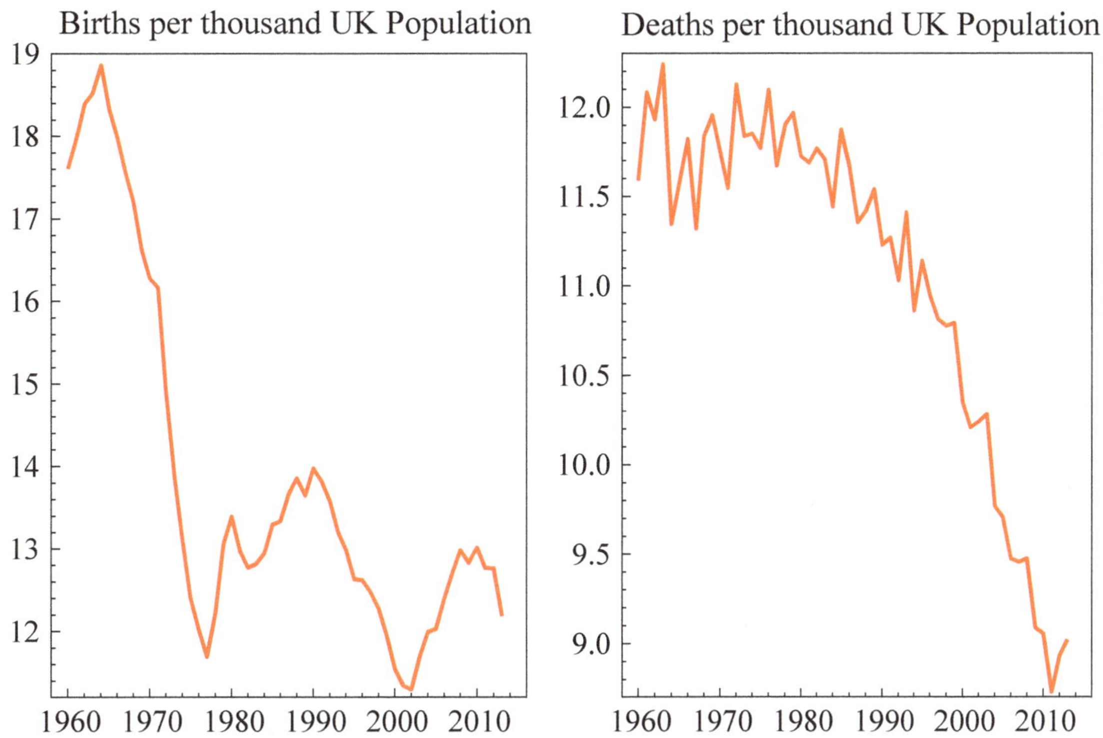

Fig. 2.3 Births and deaths per thousand of the UK population

historical dates of the observations: whether it was 1860–1895 or 1960–1995 would be essentially irrelevant.

As a corollary, a non-stationary process is one where the distribution of a variable does not stay the same at different points in time–the mean and/or variance changes–which can happen for many reasons. Stationarity is the exception and non-stationarity is the norm for most social science and environmental times series. Specific events can matter greatly, including major wars, pandemics, and massive volcanic eruptions; financial innovation; key discoveries like vaccination, antibiotics and birth control; inventions like the steam engine, dynamo and flight; etc. These can cause persistent shifts in the means and variances of the data, thereby violating stationarity. Figure 2.3 shows the large drop in UK birth rates following the introduction of oral contraception, and the large declines in death rates since 1960 due to increasing longevity. Comparing the two panels shows that births exceeded deaths at every date, so the UK population must have grown even before net immigration is taken into account.

Economies evolve and change over time in both real and nominal terms, sometimes dramatically as in major wars, the US Great Depression after 1929, the 'Oil Crises' of the mid 1970s, or the more recent 'Financial Crisis and Great Recession' over 2008–2012.

Sources of Non-stationarity

There are two important sources of non-stationarity often visible in time series: evolution and sudden shifts. The former reflects slower changes, such as knowledge accumulation and its embodiment in capital equipment, whereas the latter occurs from (e.g.) wars, major geological events, and policy regime changes. The first source is the cumulation of past shocks, somewhat akin to changes in DNA cumulating over time to permanently change later inherited characteristics. Evolution results from cumulated shocks, and that also applies to economic and other time series, making their means and variances change over time. The second source is the occurrence of sudden, often unanticipated, shifts in the level of a time series, called location shifts. The historical track record of economic forecasting is littered with forecasts that went badly wrong, an outcome that should occur infrequently in a stationary process, as then the future would be like the past. The four panels of Fig. 2.4 illustrate both such non-stationarities.

Panel (a) records US annual constant-price per capita food expenditure from 1929–2006 which has more than doubled, but at greatly varying rates manifested by the changing slopes of the line, with several major 'bumps'. Panel (b) reports the rates of price inflation workers faced: relatively stable till 1914, then rising and falling by around 20% per annum during and immediately after the First World War, peaking again during the oil crises of the 1970s before returning to a relatively stable trajectory. In Panel (c) real oil prices in constant price dollars fell for almost a century with intermittent temporary upturns before their dramatic revival in the Oil Crises that started the UK's 1970s inflation, with greatly increased volatility. Finally, Panel (d) records both the UK's coal output (dashed line) and its CO_2 emissions (solid line), both in Mt per annum: what goes up can come down. The fall in the former from 250 Mt per annum to near zero is as dramatic a non-stationarity as one could imagine, as is the behaviour of emissions, with huge 'outliers' in the 1920s and a similar '∩'

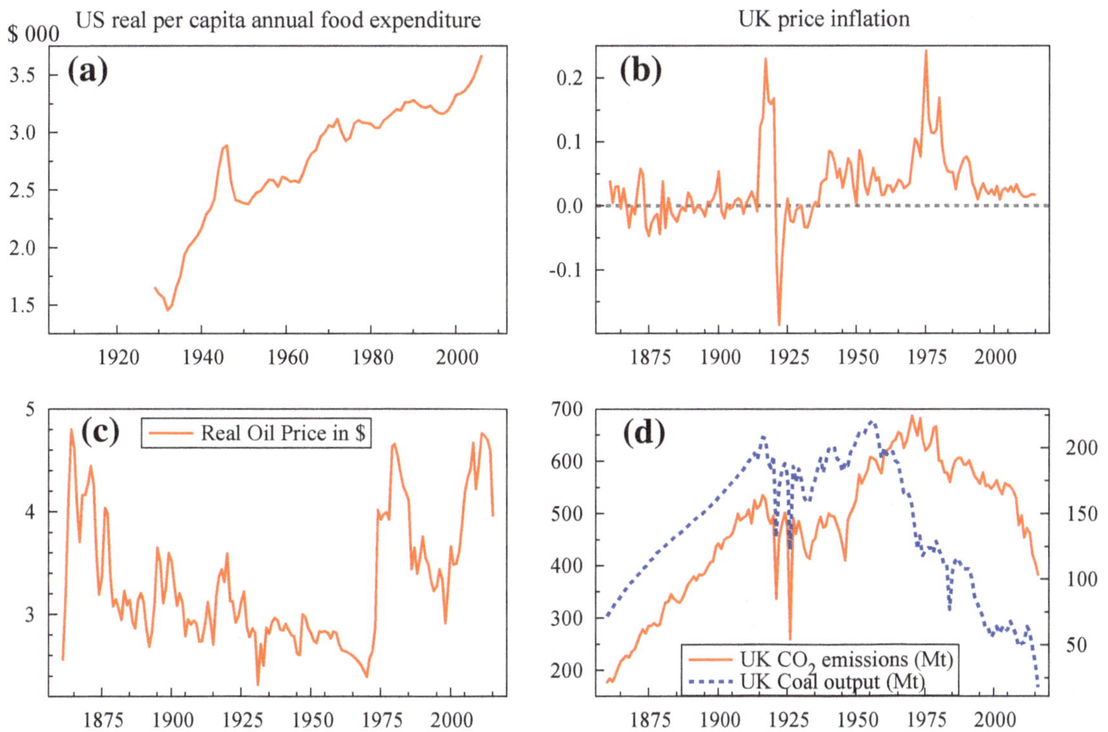

Fig. 2.4 (**a**) US real per capita annual food expenditure in $000; (**b**) UK price inflation; (**c**) Real oil price in $ (log scale); (**d**) UK coal output (right-hand axis) and CO_2 emissions (left-hand axis), both in millions of tons (Mt) per annum

shape. In per capita terms, the UK's CO_2 emissions are now below any level since 1860–when the UK was the workshop of the world.

An important source of non-stationarity is that due to what are called processes with unit roots. Such processes are highly persistent as they cumulate past shocks. Indeed, today's value of the time series equals the previous value plus the new shock: i.e., there is a unit parameter linking the successive values. Figure 2.5(a) shows the time series that results from cumulating the random numbers in Fig. 2.1(b), which evolves slowly downwards in this instance, but could 'wander' in any direction. Next, Fig. 2.5(b) records the resulting correlations between successive values, quite unlike that in Fig. 2.2(b). Even for observations 20 periods apart, the correlation is still large and positive.

Empirical modelling relating variables faces important difficulties when time series are non-stationary. If two *unrelated* time series are non-stationary because they evolve by accumulating past shocks, their cor-

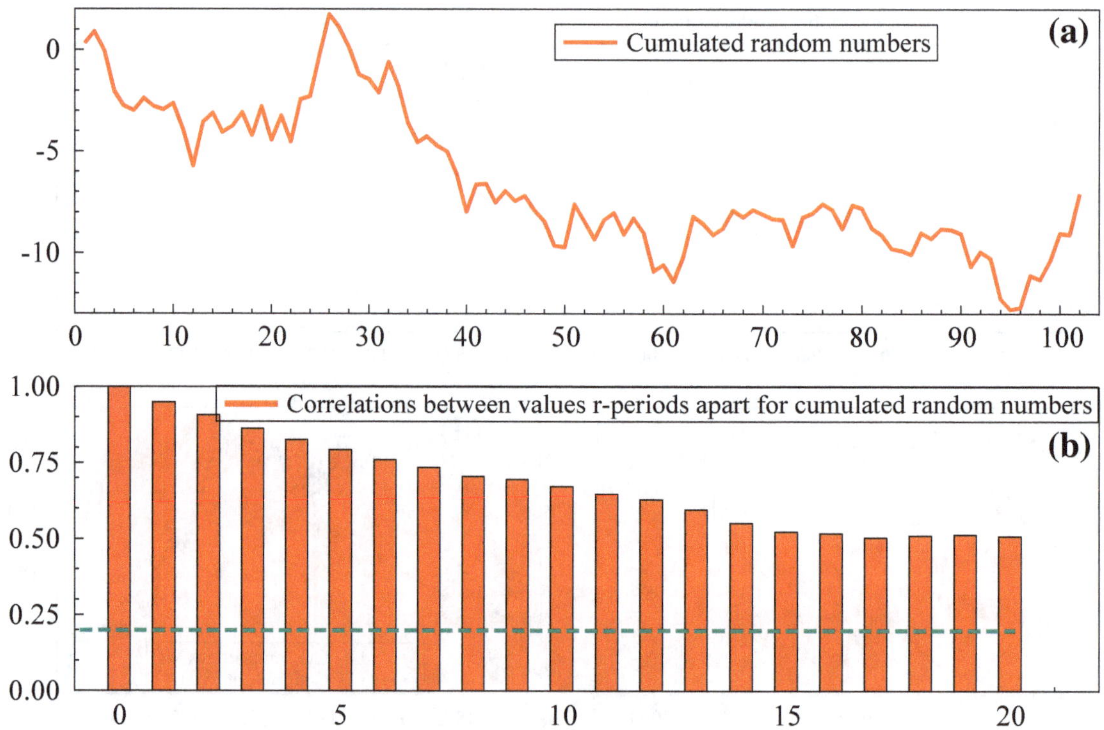

Fig. 2.5 (**a**) Time series of the cumulated random numbers; (**b**) correlations between successively futher apart observations

relation will nevertheless appear to be significant about 70% of the time using a conventional 5% decision rule.

Apocryphal examples during the Victorian era were the surprising high positive correlations between the numbers of human births and storks nesting in Stockholm, and between murders and membership of the Church of England. As a consequence, these are called nonsense relations. A silly example is shown in Fig. 2.6(a) where the global atmospheric concentrations of CO_2 are 'explained' by the monthly UK Retail Price Index (RPI), partly because both have increased over the sample, 1988(3) to 2011(6). However, Panel (b) shows that the changes in the two series are essentially unrelated.

The nonsense relations problem arises because uncertainty is seriously under-estimated if stationarity is wrongly assumed. During the 1980s, econometricians established solutions to this problem, and en-route also showed that the structure of economic behaviour virtually ensured that most economic data would be non-stationary. At first sight, this poses many difficulties for modelling economic data. But we can use it to

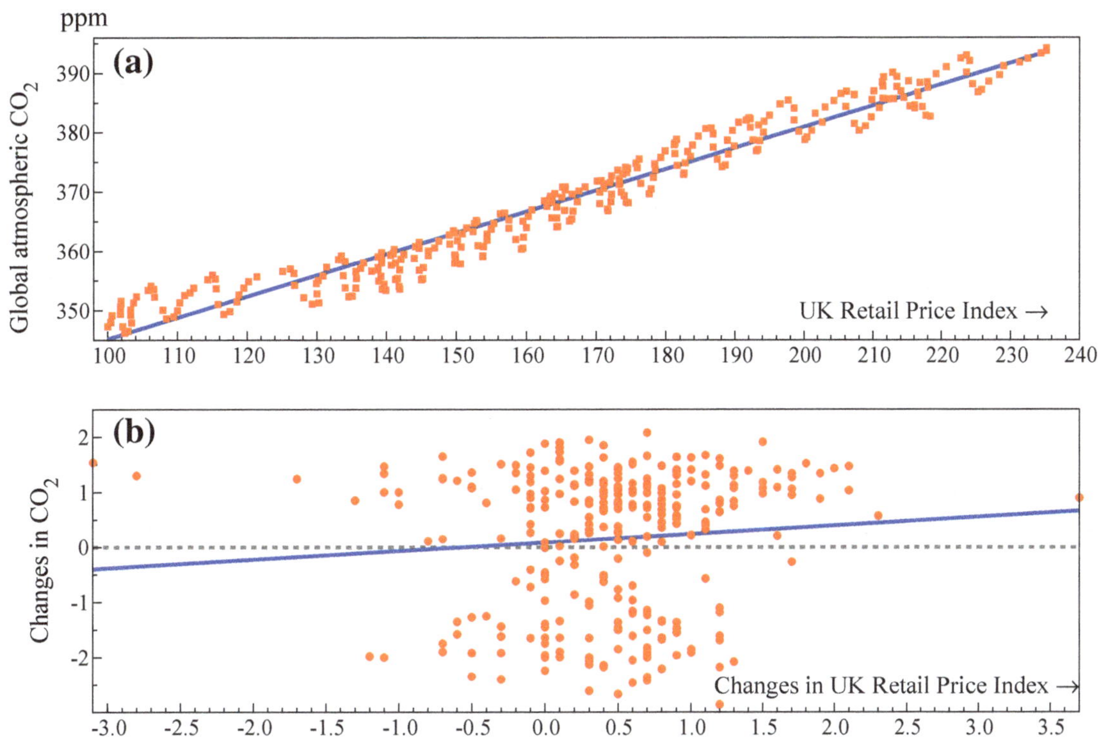

Fig. 2.6 (**a**) 'Explaining' global levels of atmospheric CO_2 by the UK retail price index (RPI); (**b**) no relation between their changes

our advantage as such non-stationarity is often accompanied by common trends. Most people make many more decisions (such as buying numerous items of shopping), than the small number of variables that guide their decisions (e.g., their income or bank balance). That non-stationary data often move closely together due to common variables driving economic decisions enables us to model the non-stationarities. Below, we will use the behaviour of UK wages, prices, productivity and unemployment over 1860–2016 to illustrate the discussion and explain empirical modelling methods that handle non-stationarities which arise from cumulating shocks.

Many economic models used in empirical research, forecasting or for guiding policy have been predicated on treating observed data as stationary. But policy decisions, empirical research and forecasting also must take the non-stationarity of the data into account if they are to deliver useful outcomes. We will offer guidance for policy makers and researchers on identifying what forms of non-stationarity are prevalent, what hazards each form implies for empirical modelling and forecasting, and for any resulting policy decisions, and what tools are available to overcome such hazards.

Historical Review of Understanding Non-stationarity

Developing a viable analysis of non-stationarity in economics really commenced with the discovery of the problem of 'nonsense correlations'. These high correlations are found between variables that should be unrelated: for example, that between the price level in the UK and cumulative annual rainfall shown in Hendry (1980).[3] Yule (1897) had considered the possibility that both variables in a correlation calculation might be related to a third variable (e.g., population growth), inducing a spuriously high correlation: this partly explains the close relation in Fig. 2.6. But by Yule (1926), he recognised the problem was indeed 'nonsense correlations'. He suspected that high correlations between successive values of variables, called serial, or auto, correlation as in Fig. 2.5(b), might affect the correlations between variables. He investigated that in a manual simulation experiment, randomly drawing from a hat pieces of paper with digits written on them. He calculated correlations between pairs of draws for many samples of those numbers and also between pairs after the numbers for each variable were cumulated once, and finally cumulated twice. For example, if the digits for the first variable went 5, 9, 1, 4, . . ., the cumulative numbers would be 5, 14, 15, 19, . . . and so on. Yule found that in the purely random case, the correlation coefficient was almost normally distributed around zero, but after the digits were cumulated once, he was surprised to find the correlation coefficient was nearly uniformly distributed, so almost all correlation values were equally likely despite there being no genuine relation between the variables. Thus, he found 'significant', though not very high, correlations far more often than for non-cumulated samples. Yule was even more startled to discover that the correlation coefficient had a U-shaped distribution when the numbers were doubly cumulated, so the correct hypothesis of no relation between the genuinely unrelated variables was virtually always rejected due to a near-perfect, yet nonsense, correlation of ± 1.

[3] Extensive histories of econometrics are provided by Morgan (1990), Qin (1993, 2013), and Hendry and Morgan (1995).

Granger and Newbold (1974) re-emphasized that an apparently 'significant relation' between variables, but where there remained substantial serial correlation in the residuals from that relation, was a symptom associated with nonsense regressions. Phillips (1986) provided a technical analysis of the sources and symptoms of nonsense regressions. Today, Yule's three types of time series are called integrated of order zero, one, and two respectively, usually denoted I(0), I(1), and I(2), as the number of times the series integrate (i.e., cumulate) past values. Conversely, differencing successive values of an I(1) series delivers an I(0) time series, etc., but loses any information connecting the levels. At the same time as Yule, Smith (1926) had already suggested that a solution was nesting models in levels and differences, but this great step forward was quickly forgotten (see Terence Mills 2011). Indeed, differencing is not the only way to reduce the order of integration of a group of related time series, as Granger (1981) demonstrated with the introduction of the concept of cointegration, extended by Engle and Granger (1987) and discussed in Sect. 4.2: see Hendry (2004) for a history of the development of cointegration.

The history of structural breaks–the topic of the next 'primer'–has been less studied, but major changes in variables and consequential shifts between relationships date back to at least the forecast failures that wrecked the embryonic US forecasting industry (see Friedman 2014). In considering forecasting the outcome for 1929–what a choice of year!–Smith (1929) foresaw the major difficulty as being unanticipated location shifts (although he used different terminology), but like his other important contribution just noted, this insight also got forgotten. Forecast failure has remained a recurrent theme in economics with notable disasters around the time of the oil crises (see e.g., Perron 1989) and the 'Great Recession' considered in Sect. 7.3.

What seems to have taken far longer to realize is that to every forecast failure there is an associated theory failure as emphasized by Hendry and Mizon (2014), an important issue we will return to in Sect. 4.4.[4] Meantime, we consider the other main form of non-stationarity, namely the many forms of 'structural breaks'.

[4]See http://www.voxeu.org/article/why-standard-macro-models-fail-crises for a less technical explanation.

2.3 Structural Breaks

What are structural breaks?

Types of structural breaks
Causes of structural breaks
Consequences of structural breaks
Tests for structural breaks
Modelling facing structural breaks
Forecasting in processes with structural breaks
Regime-shift models

Types of Structural Breaks

A *structural break* denotes a shift in the behaviour of a variable over time, such as a jump in the money stock, or a change in a previous relationship between observable variables, such as between inflation and unemployment, or the balance of trade and the exchange rate. Many sudden changes, particularly when unanticipated, cause links between variables to shift. This is a problem that is especially prevalent in economics as many structural breaks are induced by events outside the purview of most economic analyses, but examples abound in the sciences and social sciences, e.g., volcanic eruptions, earthquakes, and the discovery of penicillin. The consequences of not taking breaks into account include poor models, large forecast errors after the break, mis-guided policy, and inappropriate tests of theories.

Such breaks can take many forms. The simplest to visualize is a shift in the mean of a variable as shown in the left-hand panel of Fig. 2.7. This is a 'location shift', from a mean of zero to 2. Forecasts based on the zero mean will be systematically badly wrong.

Next, a shift in the variance of a time series is shown in the right-hand graph of Fig. 2.7. The series is fairly 'flat' till about observation 19, then varies considerably more after.

Of course, both means and variances can shift, more than once and at different times. Such shifts in a variable can also be viewed through changes in its distribution as in Fig. 2.8. Both breaks have noticeable effects if the before–after distributions are plotted together as shown. For

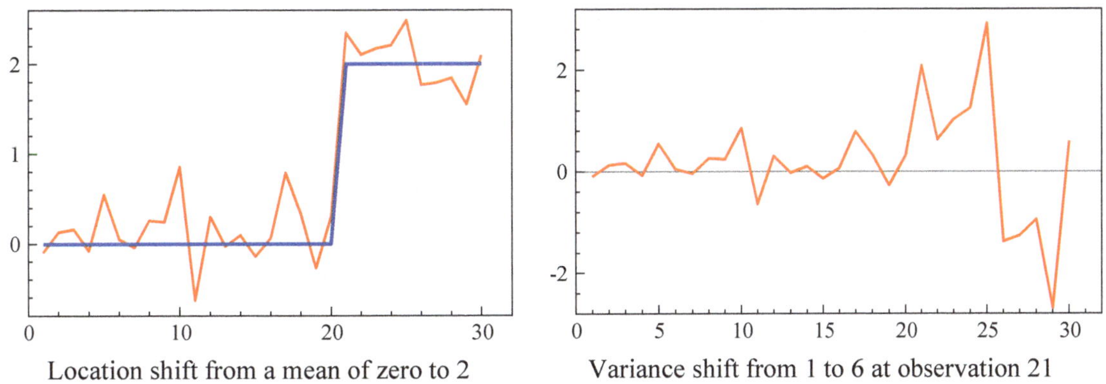

Fig. 2.7 Two examples of structural breaks

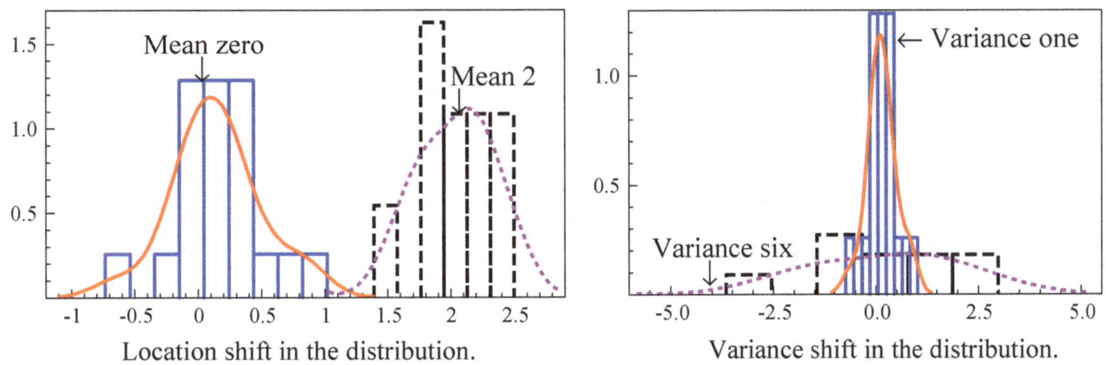

Fig. 2.8 The impacts on the statistical distributions of the two examples of structural breaks

a location shift, the entire distribution is moved to a new center; for a variance increase, it remains centered as before but much more spread.

Distributional shifts certainly occur in the real world, as Fig. 2.9 shows, plotting four sub-periods of annual UK CO_2 emissions in Mt. The first three sub-periods all show the centers of the distributions moving to higher values, but the fourth (1980–2016) jumps back below the previous sub-period distribution.

Shifts in just one variable in a relationship causes their link to break. In the left-hand graph of Fig. 2.10, the dependent variable has a location shift, but the explanatory variable does not: separate fits are quite unlike the overall fit. In the right-hand graph of Fig. 2.10, the regression slope parameter changes from 1 to 2. Combinations of breaks in means, variances, trends and slopes can also occur. Naturally, such combinations can be very difficult to unravel empirically.

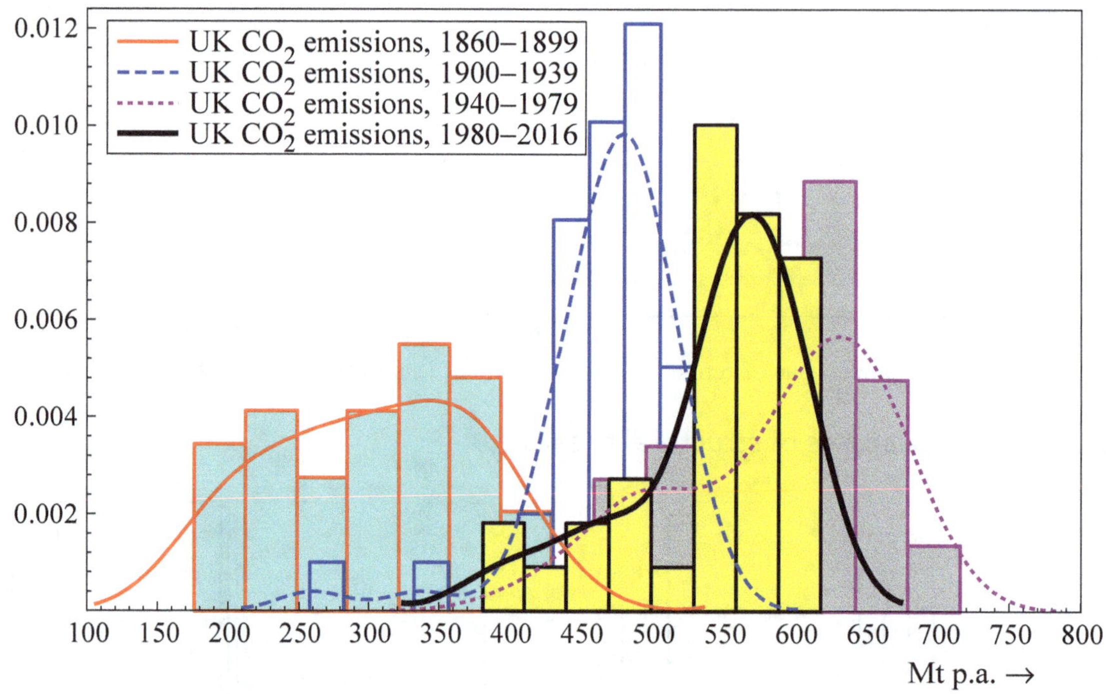

Fig. 2.9 Distributional shifts of total UK CO_2 emissions, Mt p.a.

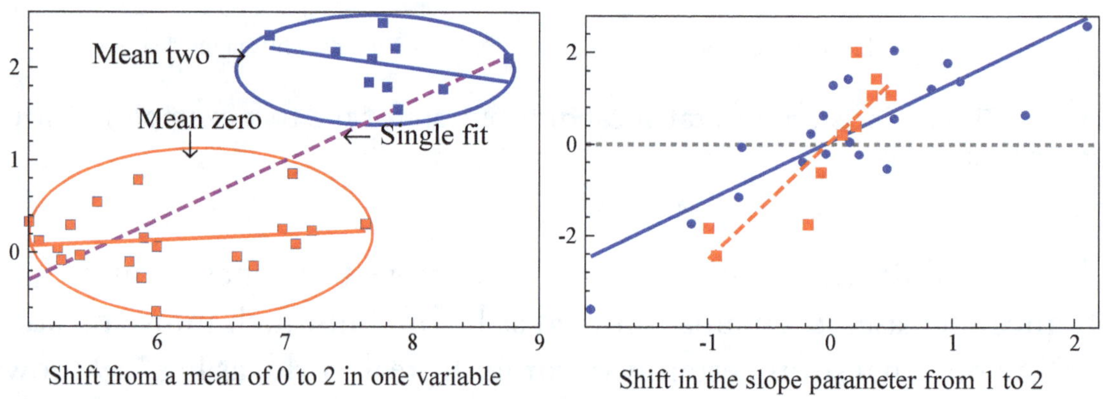

Fig. 2.10 The impacts on statistical relationships of shifts in mean and slope parameters

Causes of Structural Breaks

The world has changed enormously in almost every measurable way over the last few centuries, sometimes abruptly (for a large body of evidence, see the many time series in https://ourworldindata.org/). Of the numerous possible instances, dramatic shifts include World War I; the 1918–20 flu' epidemic; 1929 crash and ensuing Great Depression; World War II; the 1970s oil crises; 1997 Asian financial crisis; the 2000 'dot com' crash; and the 2008–2012 financial crisis and Great Recession (and maybe Brexit). Such large and sudden breaks usually lead to location shifts. More gradual changes can cause the parameters of relationships to 'drift': changes in technology, social mores, or legislation usually take time to work through.

Consequences of Structural Breaks

The impacts of structural breaks on empirical models naturally depend on their forms, magnitudes, and numbers, as well as on how well specified the model in question is. When large location shifts or major changes in the parameters linking variables in a relationship are not handled correctly, statistical estimates of relations will be distorted. As we discuss in Chapter 7, this often leads to forecast failure, and if the 'broken' relation is used for policy, the outcomes of policy interventions will not be as expected. Thus, viable relationships need to account for all the structural breaks that occurred, even though in practice, there will be an unknown number, most of which will have an unknown magnitude, form, and duration and may even have unknown starting and ending dates.

Tests for Structural Breaks

There are many tests for structural breaks in given relationships, but these often depend not only on knowing the correct relationship to be tested, but also on knowing a considerable amount about the types of breaks, and the properties of the time series being analyzed. Tests include those proposed by Brown et al. (1975), Chow (1960), Nyblom (1989), Hansen (1992a), Hansen (1992b) (for I(1) data), Jansen and Teräsvirta (1996), and Bai and Perron (1998, 2003). Perron (2006) provided a wide ranging survey of then available methods of estimation and testing in models with structural breaks, including their close links to processes with unit roots, which are non-stationary stochastic processes (discussed above) that can cause problems in statistical inference. To apply any test requires that the model is already specified, so while it is certainly wise to test if there are important structural breaks leading to parameter non-constancies, their discovery then reveals the model to be flawed, and how to 'repair' it is always unclear. Tests can reject because of other untreated problems than the one for which they were designed: for example, apparent non-constancy may be due to residual autocorrelation, or unmodelled persistence left in the unexplained component, which distorts the estimated standard errors (see e.g., Corsi et al. 1982). A break can occur because an omitted determinant shifts, or from a location shift in an irrelevant variable included inadvertently, and the 'remedy' naturally differs between such settings.

Modelling Facing Structural Breaks

Failing to model breaks will almost always lead to a badly-specified empirical model that will not usefully represent the data. Knowing of or having detected breaks, a common approach is to 'model' them by adding appropriate indicator variables, namely artificial variables that are zero for most of a sample period but unity over the time that needs to be indicated as having a shift: Fig. 2.7 illustrates a step indicator that takes the value 2 for observations 21–30. Indicators can be formulated to reflect any relevant aspect of a model, such as changing trends, or multiplied by variables to capture when parameters shift, and so on. It is possible to design *model selection* strategies that tackle structural breaks automatically as part of their algorithm, as advocated by Hendry and Doornik (2014). Even though such approaches, called indicator saturation methods (see Johansen and Nielsen 2009; Castle et al. 2015), lead to more candidate explanatory variables than there are available observations, it is possible for a model selection algorithm to include large blocks of indicators for any number of outliers and location shifts, and even parameter changes (see e.g., Ericsson 2012). Indicators relevant to the problem at hand can be designed in advance, as with the approach used to detect the impacts of volcanic eruptions on temperature in Pretis et al. (2016).

Forecasting in Processes with Structural Breaks

In the forecasting context, not all structural breaks matter equally, and indeed some have essentially no effect on forecast accuracy, but may change the precision of forecasts, or estimates of forecast-error variances. Clements and Hendry (1998) provide a taxonomy of sources of forecast errors which explains why location shifts—changes in the previous means, or levels, of variables in relationships—are the main cause of forecast failures. Ericsson (1992) provides a clear discussion. Figure 2.7 again illustrates why the previous mean provides a very poor forecast of the final 10 data points. Rapid detection of such shifts, or better still, forecasting them in advance, can reduce systematic forecast failure, as can a number of devices for robustifying forecasts after location shifts, such as intercept corrections and additional differencing, the topic of Chapter 7.

Regime-Shift Models

An alternative approach models shifts, including recessions, as the outcome of stochastic shocks in non-linear dynamic processes, the large literature on which was partly surveyed by Hamilton (2016). Such models assume there is a probability at any point in time, conditional on the current regime and possibly several recent past regimes, that an economy might switch to a different state. A range of models have been proposed that could characterize such processes, which Hamilton describes as 'a rich set of tools and specifications on which to draw for interpreting data and building economic models for environments in which there may be changes in regime'. However, an important concern is which specification and which tools apply in any given instance, and how to choose between them when a given model formulation is not guaranteed to be fully appropriate. Consequently, important selection and evaluation issues must be addressed.

2.4 Model Selection

Why do we need model selection?

- **What is model selection?**
- **Evaluating empirical models**
- **Objectives of model selection**
- **Model selection methods**
- **Concepts used in analyses of statistical model selection**
- **Consequences of statistical model selection**

What is Model Selection?

Model selection concerns choosing a formal representation of a set of data from a range of possible specifications thereof. It is ubiquitous in observational-data studies because the processes generating the data are almost never known. How selection is undertaken is sometimes not described, and may even give the impression that the final model reported was the first to be fitted. When the number of candidate variables needing analyzed is larger than the available sample, selection is inevitable as the complete model cannot be estimated. In general, the choice of selection method depends on the nature of the problem being addressed and the purpose for which a model is being sought, and can be seen as an aspect of testing multiple hypotheses: see Lehmann (1959). Purposes include understanding links between data series (especially how they evolved over the past), to test a theory, to forecast future outcomes, and (in e.g., economics and climatology) to conduct policy analyses.

It might be thought that a single 'best' model (on some criteria) should resolve all four purposes, but that transpires not to be the case, especially when observational data are not stationary. Indeed, the set of models from which one is to be selected may be implicit, as when the functional form of the relation under study is not known (linear, log-linear or non-linear), or when there may be an unknown number of outliers, or even shifts. Model selection can also apply to the design of experiments such that the data collected is well-suited to the problem. As Konishi and Kitagawa (2008, p. 75) state, 'The majority of the problems in statistical inference can be considered to be problems related to statistical modeling'. Relatedly, Sir David Cox (2006, p. 197) has said, 'How [the] translation from subject-matter problem to statistical model is done is often the most critical part of an analysis'.

Evaluating Empirical Models

Irrespective of how models are selected, it is always feasible to evaluate any chosen model against the available empirical evidence. There are two main criteria for doing so in our approach, *congruence* and *encompassing*.

The first concerns how well the model fits the data, the theory and any constraints imposed by the nature of the observations. Fitting the data requires that the unexplained components, or residuals, match the properties assumed for the errors in the model formulation. These usually entail no systematic behaviour, such as successive residuals being correlated (serial or autocorrelation), that the residuals are relatively homogeneous in their variability (called homoscedastic), and that all parameters which are assumed to be constant over time actually are. Matching the theory requires that the model formulation is consistent with the analysis from which it is derived, but does not require that the theory model is imposed on the data, both because abstract theory may not reflect the underlying behaviour, and because little would be learned if empirical results merely put ragged cloth on a sketchy theory skeleton. Matching intrinsic data properties may involve taking logarithms to ensure an inherently positive variable is modelled as such, or that flows cumulate correctly to stocks, and that outcomes satisfy accounting constraints.

Although satisfying all of these requirements may seem demanding, there are settings in which they are all trivially satisfied. For example, if the data are all orthogonal, and independent identically distributed (IID)—such as independent draws from a Normal distribution with a constant mean and variance and no data constraints—all models would appear to be congruent with whatever theory was used in their formulation. Thus, an additional criterion is whether a model can encompass, or explain the results of, rival explanations of the same variables. There is a large literature on alternative approaches, but the simplest is parsimonious encompassing in which an empirical model is embedded within the most general formulation (often the union of all the contending models) and loses no significant information relative to that general model. In the orthogonal IID setting just noted, a congruent model may be found wanting because some variables it excluded are highly significant statistically when included. That example also emphasizes that congruence is not definitive, and most certainly is not 'truth', in that a sequence of successively encompassing congruent empirical models can be developed in a progressive research strategy: see Mizon (1984, 2008), Hendry (1988, 1995), Govaerts et al. (1994), Hoover and Perez (1999), Bontemps and Mizon (2003, 2008), and Doornik (2008).

Objectives of Model Selection

At base, selection is an attempt to find all the relevant determinants of a phenomenon usually represented by measurements on a variable, or set of variables, of interest, while eliminating all the influences that are irrelevant for the problem at hand. This is most easily understood for relationships between variables where some are to be 'explained' as functions of others, but it is not known which of the potential 'explaining' variables really matter. A simple strategy to ensure all relevant variables are retained is to always keep every candidate variable; whereas to ensure no irrelevant variables are retained, keep no variables at all. Manifestly these strategies conflict, but highlight the 'trade-off' that affects all selection approaches: the more likely a method is to retain relevant influences by some criterion (such as statistical significance) the more likely some irrelevant influences will chance to be retained. The costs and benefits of that trade-off depend on the context, the approach adopted, the sample size, the numbers of irrelevant and relevant variables—which are unknown—how substantive the latter are, as well as on the purpose of the analysis.

For reliably testing a theory, the model must certainly include all the theory-relevant variables, but also all the variables that in fact affect the outcomes being modelled, whereas little damage may be done by also including some variables that are not actually relevant. However, for forecasting, even estimating the in-sample process that generated the data need not produce the forecasts with the smallest mean-square errors (see e.g., Clements and Hendry 1998). Finally, for policy interventions, it is essential that the relation between target and instrument is causal, and that the parameters of the model in use are also invariant to the intervention if the policy change is to have the anticipated effect. Here the key concept is of invariance under changes, so shifts in the policy variable, say a price rise intended to increase revenue from sales, does not alter consumers' attitudes to the company in question, thereby shifting their demand functions and so leading to the unintended consequence of a more than proportionate fall in sales.

Model Selection Methods

Most empirical models are selected by some process, varying from imposing a theory-model on the data evidence (having 'selected' the theory), through manual choice, which may be to suit an investigator's preferences, to when a computer algorithm such as machine learning is used. Even in this last case, there is a large range of possible approaches, as well as many choices as to how each algorithm functions, and the different settings in which each algorithm is likely to work well or badly—as many are likely to do for non-stationary data. The earliest selection approaches were manual as no other methods were on offer, but most of the decisions made during selection were then undocumented (see the critique in Leamer 1978), making replication difficult. In economics, early selection criteria were based on the 'goodness-of-fit' of models, pejoratively called 'data mining', but Gilbert (1986) highlighted that a greater danger of selection was its being used to suppress conflicting evidence. Statistical analyses of selection methods have provided many insights: e.g., Anderson (1962) established the dominance of testing from the most general specification and eliminating irrelevant variables relative to starting from the simplest and retaining significant ones. The long list of possible methods includes, but is not restricted to, the following, most of which use parsimony (in the sense of penalizing larger models) as part of their choice criteria.

Information criteria have a long history as a method of choosing between alternative models. Various information criteria have been proposed, all of which aim to choose between competing models by selecting the model with the smallest information loss. The trade-off between information loss and model 'complexity' is captured by the penalty, which differs between information criteria. For example, the AIC proposed by Akaike (1973), sought to balance the costs when forecasting from a stationary infinite autoregression of estimation variance from retaining small effects against the squared bias of omitting them. Schwarz (1978) SIC (also called BIC, for Bayesian information criterion), aimed to consistently estimate the parameters of a fixed, finite-dimensional model as the sample size increased to infinity. HQ, from Hannan and Quinn (1979), established the smallest penalty function that will deliver the same outcome as SIC in very large samples. Other variants of information criteria include focused criteria (see Claeskens and Hjort 2003), and the posterior information criterion in Phillips and Ploberger (1996).

Variants of **selection by goodness of fit** include choosing by the maximum multiple correlation coefficient (criticised by Lovell 1983); Mallows (1973) C_p criterion; step-wise regression (see e.g., Derksen and Keselman 1992, which Leamer called 'unwise'), which is a class of single-path search procedures for (usually) adding variables one at a time to a regression (e.g., including the next variable with the highest remaining correlation), only retaining significant estimated parameters, or dropping the least significant remaining variables in turn.

Penalised-fit approaches like shrinkage estimators, as in James and Stein (1961), and the Lasso (least absolute shrinkage and selection operator) proposed by Tibshirani (1996) and Efron et al. (2004). These are like step-wise with an additional penalty for each extra parameter.

Bayesian selection methods which often lead to model averaging: see Raftery (1995), Phillips (1995), Buckland et al. (1997), Burnham and Anderson (2002), and Hoeting et al. (1999), and Bayesian structural time series (BSTS: Scott and Varian 2014).

Automated general-to-specific (Gets) approaches as in Hoover and Perez (1999), Hendry and Krolzig (2001), Doornik (2009), and Hendry and Doornik (2014). This approach will be the one mainly used in this book when we need to explicitly select a model from a larger set of candidates, especially when there are more such candidates than the number of observations.

Model selection also has many different designations, such as subset selection (Miller 2002), and may include computer learning algorithms.

Concepts for analyses of statistical model selection

There are also many different concepts employed in the analyses of statistical methods of model selection. Retention of irrelevant variables is often measured by the 'false-positives rate' or 'false-discovery rate' namely, how often irrelevant variables are incorrectly selected by a test adventitiously rejecting the null hypothesis of irrelevance. If a test is correctly calibrated (which unfortunately is often not the case for many methods of model selection, such as step-wise), and has a nominal significance level of (say) 1%, it should reject the null hypothesis incorrectly 1% of the time (Type-I error). Thus, if 100 such tests are conducted under the null, 1 should reject by chance on average (i.e., 100×0.01). Hendry and Doornik (2014) refer to the actual retention rate of irrelevant variables during selection as the empirical gauge and seek to calibrate their algorithm such that the gauge is close to the nominal significance level. Johansen and Nielsen (2016) investigate the distribution of estimates of the gauge. Bayesian approaches often focus on the concept of 'model uncertainty', essentially the probability of selecting closely similar models that nevertheless lead to different conclusions. With 100 candidate variables, there are $2^{100} \approx 10^{30}$ possible models generated by every combination of the 100 variables, creating great scope for such model uncertainty. Nevertheless, when all variables are irrelevant, on average 1 variable would be retained at 1%, so model uncertainty has been hugely reduced from a gigantic set of possibilities to a tiny number. Although different irrelevant variables will be selected adventitiously in different draws, this is hardly a useful concept of 'model uncertainty'.

The more pertinent difficulty is finding and retaining relevant variables, which depends on how substantive their influence is. If a variable would not be retained by the criterion in use even when it was the known sole relevant variable, it will usually not be retained by selection from a larger set. Crucially, a relevant variable can only be retained if it is in the candidate set being considered, so indicators for outliers and shifts will never be found unless they are considered. One strategy is to always retain the set of variables entailed by the theory that motivated the analysis while selecting from other potential determinants, shift effects etc., allowing model discovery jointly with evaluating the theory (see Hendry and Doornik 2014).

Consequences of Statistical Model Selection

Selection of course affects the statistical properties of the resulting estimated model, usually because only effects that are 'significant' at the prespecified level are retained. Thus, which variables are selected varies in different samples and on average, estimated coefficients of retained relevant variables are biased away from the origin. Retained irrelevant variables are those that chanced to have estimated coefficients far from zero in the particular data sample. The former are often called 'pre-test biases' as in Judge and Bock (1978). The top panel in Fig. 2.11 illustrates when $\widehat{b}$ denotes the distribution without selection, and $\widetilde{b}$ with selection requiring

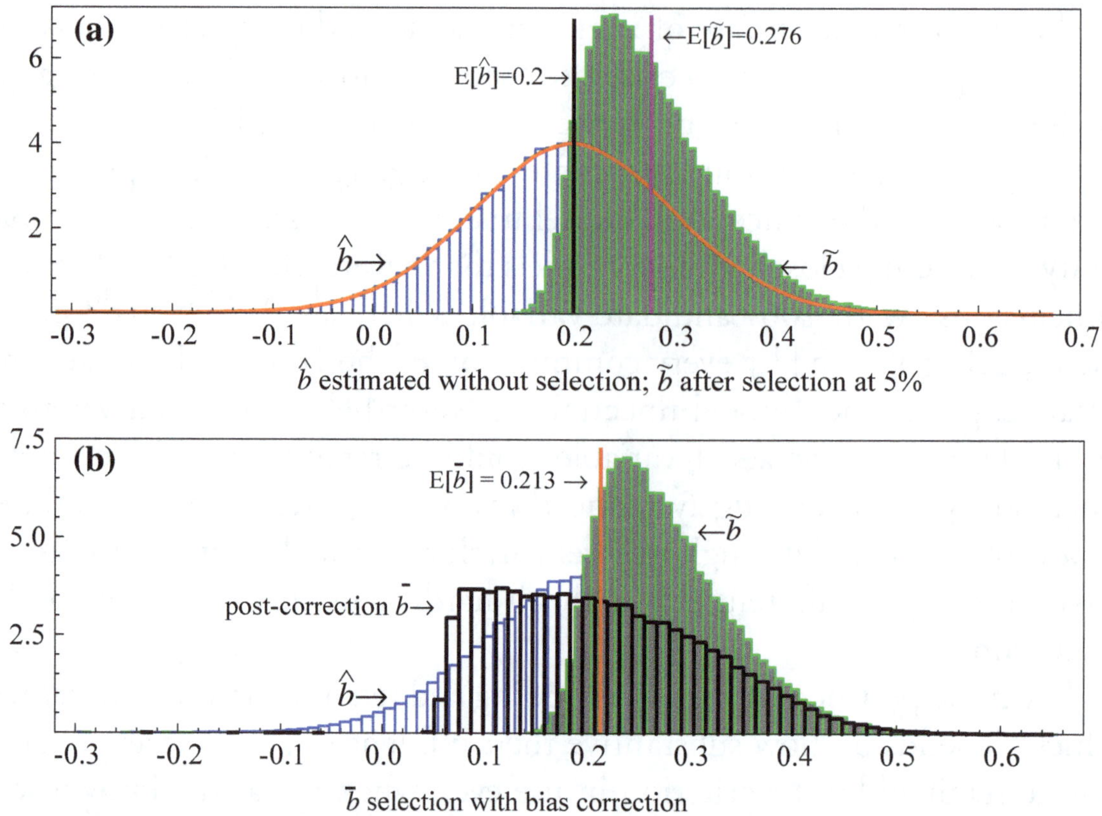

Fig. 2.11 **(a)** The impact on the statistical distributions of selecting only significant parameters; **(b)** distributions after bias correction

significance at 5%. The latter distribution is shifted to the right and has a mean $\mathsf{E}[\widetilde{b}]$ of 0.276 when the unselected mean $\mathsf{E}[\widehat{b}]$ is 0.2, leading to an upward bias of 38%.

However, if coefficients of relevant variables are highly significant, such selection biases are small. In some settings, such biases can be corrected after selection in well-structured algorithms, as shown by Hendry and Krolzig (2005). The lower panel in Fig. 2.11 illustrates the effect of bias correction on the distribution of $\widetilde{b}$ to $\overline{b}$. There is a strong shift back to the left, and the corrected mean is 0.213, so now is only slightly biased. The same bias corrections applied to the coefficients of irrelevant variables that are retained by chance can considerably reduce their mean-square errors.

A more important issue is that omitting relevant variables will bias the remaining retained coefficients (except if all variables are mutually orthogonal), and that effect will often be far larger than selection biases, and cannot be corrected as it is not known which omitted variables are relevant.

Of course, simply asserting a relation and estimating it without selection is likely to be even more prone to such biases unless an investigator is omniscient. In almost every observational discipline, especially those facing non-stationary data, selection is inevitable. Consequently, the least-worst route is to allow for as many potentially relevant explanatory variables as feasible to avoid omitted-variables biases, and use an automatic selection approach, aka a machine-learning algorithm, balancing the costs of over and under inclusion. Hence, Campos et al. (2005) focus on methods that commence from the most general feasible specification and conduct simplification searches leading to three generations of automatic selection algorithms in the sequence Hoover and Perez (1999), *PcGets* by Hendry and Krolzig (2001) and *Autometrics* by Doornik (2009), embedded in the approach to model discovery by Hendry and Doornik (2014). We now consider the prevalence of non-stationarity in observational data.

References

Akaike, H. (1973). Information theory and an extension of the maximum likelihood principle. In Petrov, B. N., and Csaki, F. (eds.), *Second International Symposion on Information Theory*, pp. 267–281. Budapest: Akademia Kiado.

Anderson, T. W. (1962). The choice of the degree of a polynomial regression as a multiple-decision problem. *Annals of Mathematical Statistics*, **33**, 255–265.

Bai, J., and Perron, P. (1998). Estimating and testing linear models with multiple structural changes. *Econometrica*, **66**, 47–78.

Bai, J., and Perron, P. (2003). Computation and analysis of multiple structural change models. *Journal of Applied Econometrics*, **18**, 1–22.

Bontemps, C., and Mizon, G. E. (2003). Congruence and encompassing. In Stigum, B. P. (ed.), *Econometrics and the Philosophy of Economics*, pp. 354–378. Princeton: Princeton University Press.

Bontemps, C., and Mizon, G. E. (2008). Encompassing: Concepts and implementation. *Oxford Bulletin of Economics and Statistics*, **70**, 721–750.

Brown, R. L., Durbin, J., and Evans, J. M. (1975). Techniques for testing the constancy of regression relationships over time (with discussion). *Journal of the Royal Statistical Society B*, **37**, 149–192.

Buckland, S. T., Burnham, K. P., and Augustin, N. H. (1997). Model selection: An integral part of inference. *Biometrics*, **53**, 603–618.

Burnham, K. P., and Anderson, D. R. (2002). *Model Selection and Multimodel Inference: A Practical Information-Theoretic Approach*, 2nd Edition. New York: Springer.

Campos, J., Ericsson, N. R., and Hendry, D. F. (2005). Editors' introduction. In Campos, J., Ericsson, N. R., and Hendry, D. F. (eds.), *Readings on General-to-Specific Modeling*, pp. 1–81. Cheltenham: Edward Elgar.

Castle, J. L., Doornik, J. A., Hendry, D. F., and Pretis, F. (2015). Detecting location shifts during model selection by step-indicator saturation. *Econometrics*, **3(2)**, 240–264. http://www.mdpi.com/2225-1146/3/2/240.

Chow, G. C. (1960). Tests of equality between sets of coefficients in two linear regressions. *Econometrica*, **28**, 591–605.

Claeskens, G., and Hjort, N. L. (2003). The focussed information criterion (with discussion). *Journal of the American Statistical Association*, **98**, 879–945.

Clements, M. P., and Hendry, D. F. (1998). *Forecasting Economic Time Series.* Cambridge: Cambridge University Press.

Corsi, P., Pollock, R. E., and Prakken, J. C. (1982). The Chow test in the presence of serially correlated errors. In Chow, G. C., and Corsi, P. (eds.), *Evaluating the Reliability of Macro-economic Models.* New York: Wiley.

Cox, D. R. (2006). *Principles of Statistical Inference.* Cambridge: Cambridge University Press.

Derksen, S., and Keselman, H. J. (1992). Backward, forward and stepwise automated subset selection algorithms: Frequency of obtaining authentic and noise variables. *British Journal of Mathematical and Statistical Psychology*, **45**, 265–282.

Doornik, J. A. (2008). Encompassing and automatic model selection. *Oxford Bulletin of Economics and Statistics*, **70**, 915–925.

Doornik, J. A. (2009). Autometrics. In Castle, J. L., and Shephard, N. (eds.), *The Methodology and Practice of Econometrics*, pp. 88–121. Oxford: Oxford University Press.

Efron, B., Hastie, T., Johnstone, I., and Tibshirani, R. (2004). Least angle regression. *The Annals of Statistics*, **32**, 407–499.

Engle, R. F., and Granger, C. W. J. (1987). Cointegration and error correction: Representation, estimation and testing. *Econometrica*, **55**, 251–276.

Ericsson, N. R. (1992). Parameter constancy, mean square forecast errors, and measuring forecast performance: An exposition, extensions, and illustration. *Journal of Policy Modeling*, **14**, 465–495.

Ericsson, N. R. (2012). Detecting crises, jumps, and changes in regime. Working paper, Federal Reserve Board of Governors, Washington, DC.

Friedman, W. A. (2014). *Fortune Tellers: The Story of America's First Economic Forecasters.* Princeton: Princeton University Press.

Gilbert, C. L. (1986). Professor Hendry's econometric methodology. *Oxford Bulletin of Economics and Statistics*, **48**, 283–307. Reprinted in Granger, C. W. J. (ed.) (1990). *Modelling Economic Series.* Oxford: Clarendon Press.

Govaerts, B., Hendry, D. F., and Richard, J.-F. (1994). Encompassing in stationary linear dynamic models. *Journal of Econometrics*, **63**, 245–270.

Granger, C. W. J. (1981). Some properties of time series data and their use in econometric model specification. *Journal of Econometrics*, **16**, 121–130.

Granger, C. W. J., and Newbold, P. (1974). Spurious regressions in econometrics. *Journal of Econometrics*, **2**, 111–120.

Hamilton, J. D. (2016). Macroeconomic regimes and regime shifts. In Taylor, J. B., and Uhlig, H. (eds.), *Handbook of Macroeconomics*, Vol. 2, pp. 163–201. Amsterdam: Elsevier.

Hannan, E. J., and Quinn, B. G. (1979). The determination of the order of an autoregression. *Journal of the Royal Statistical Society B*, **41**, 190–195.

Hansen, B. E. (1992a). Testing for parameter instability in linear models. *Journal of Policy Modeling*, **14**, 517–533.

Hansen, B. E. (1992b). Tests for parameter instability in regressions with I(1) processes. *Journal of Business and Economic Statistics*, **10**, 321–335.

Hendry, D. F. (1980). Econometrics: Alchemy or science? *Economica*, **47**, 387–406.

Hendry, D. F. (1988). Encompassing. *National Institute Economic Review*, **125**, 88–92.

Hendry, D. F. (1995). *Dynamic Econometrics.* Oxford: Oxford University Press.

Hendry, D. F. (2004). The Nobel Memorial Prize for Clive W.J. Granger. *Scandinavian Journal of Economics*, **106**, 187–213.

Hendry, D. F., and Doornik, J. A. (2014). *Empirical Model Discovery and Theory Evaluation.* Cambridge, MA: MIT Press.

Hendry, D. F., and Krolzig, H.-M. (2001). *Automatic Econometric Model Selection.* London: Timberlake Consultants Press.

Hendry, D. F., and Krolzig, H.-M. (2005). The properties of automatic Gets modelling. *Economic Journal*, **115**, C32–C61.

Hendry, D. F., and Mizon, G. E. (2014). Unpredictability in economic analysis, econometric modeling and forecasting. *Journal of Econometrics*, **182**, 186–195.

Hendry, D. F., and Morgan, M. S. (eds.) (1995). *The Foundations of Econometric Analysis.* Cambridge: Cambridge University Press.

Hoeting, J., Madigan, D., Raftery, A., and Volinsky, C. (1999). Bayesian Model Averaging: A Tutorial. *Statistical Science*, **14(4)**, 382–417.

Hoover, K. D., and Perez, S. J. (1999). Data mining reconsidered: Encompassing and the general-to-specific approach to specification search. *Econometrics Journal*, **2**, 167–191.

James, W., and Stein, C. (1961). Estimation with quadratic loss. In Neyman, J. (ed.), *Proceedings of the Fourth Berkeley Symposium on Mathematical Statistics and Probability*, pp. 361–379. Berkeley: University of California Press.

Jansen, E. S., and Teräsvirta, T. (1996). Testing parameter constancy and super exogeneity in econometric equations. *Oxford Bulletin of Economics and Statistics*, **58**, 735–763.

Johansen, S., and Nielsen, B. (2009). An analysis of the indicator saturation estimator as a robust regression estimator. In Castle, J. L., and Shephard, N. (eds.), *The Methodology and Practice of Econometrics*, pp. 1–36. Oxford: Oxford University Press.

Johansen, S., and Nielsen, B. (2016). Asymptotic theory of outlier detection algorithms for linear time series regression models. *Scandinavian Journal of Statistics*, **43**, 321–348.

Judge, G. G., and Bock, M. E. (1978). *The Statistical Implications of Pre-test and Stein-Rule Estimators in Econometrics*. Amsterdam: North Holland Publishing Company.

Konishi, S., and Kitagawa, G. (2008). *Information Criteria and Statistical Modeling*. New York: Springer.

Leamer, E. E. (1978). *Specification Searches: Ad Hoc Inference with Non-Experimental Data*. New York: Wiley.

Lehmann, E. L. (1959). *Testing Statistical Hypotheses*. New York: Wiley.

Lovell, M. C. (1983). Data mining. *Review of Economics and Statistics*, **65**, 1–12.

Mallows, C. L. (1973). Some comments on c_p. *Technometrics*, **15**, 661–675.

Miller, A. J. (ed.) (2002). *Subset Selection in Regression*, 2nd Edition. London: Chapman & Hall (1st, 1990).

Mills, T. C. (2011). Bradford Smith: An econometrician decades ahead of his time. *Oxford Bulletin of Economics and Statistics*, **73**, 276–285.

Mizon, G. E. (1984). The encompassing approach in econometrics. In Hendry, D. F., and Wallis, K. F. (eds.), *Econometrics and Quantitative Economics*, pp. 135–172. Oxford: Basil Blackwell.

Mizon, G. E. (2008). Encompassing. In Durlauf, S., and Blume, L. (eds.), *New Palgrave Dictionary of Economics*, 2nd Edition. London: Palgrave Macmillan. https://doi.org/10.1057/9780230226203.0470.

Morgan, M. S. (1990). *The History of Econometric Ideas.* Cambridge: Cambridge University Press.

Nyblom, J. (1989). Testing for the constancy of parameters over time. *Journal of the American Statistical Association*, **84**, 223–230.

Perron, P. (1989). The Great Crash, the oil price shock and the unit root hypothesis. *Econometrica*, **57**, 1361–1401.

Perron, P. (2006). Dealing with structural breaks. In Hassani, H., Mills, T. C., and Patterson, K. D. (eds.), *Palgrave Handbook of Econometrics*, pp. 278–352. Basingstoke: Palgrave MacMillan.

Phillips, P. C. B. (1986). Understanding spurious regressions in econometrics. *Journal of Econometrics*, **33**, 311–340.

Phillips, P. C. B. (1995). Bayesian model selection and prediction with empirical applications. *Journal of Econometrics*, **69**, 289–331.

Phillips, P. C. B., and Ploberger, W. (1996). An asymptotic theory of Bayesian inference for time series. *Econometrica*, **64**, 381–412.

Pretis, F., Schneider, L., Smerdon, J. E., and Hendry, D. F. (2016). Detecting volcanic eruptions in temperature reconstructions by designed break-indicator saturation. *Journal of Economic Surveys*, **30**, 403–429.

Qin, D. (1993). *The Formation of Econometrics: A Historical Perspective.* Oxford: Clarendon Press.

Qin, D. (2013). *A History of Econometrics: The Reformation from the 1970s.* Oxford: Clarendon Press.

Raftery, A. (1995). Bayesian model selection in social research. *Sociological Methodology*, **25**, 111–196.

Schwarz, G. (1978). Estimating the dimension of a model. *Annals of Statistics*, **6**, 461–464.

Scott, S. L., and Varian, H. R. (2014). Predicting the present with Bayesian structural time series. *International Journal of Mathematical Modelling and Numerical Optimisation*, **5(102)**, 4–23.

Smith, B. B. (1926). Combining the advantages of first-difference and deviation-from-trend methods of correlating time series. *Journal of the American Statistical Association*, **21**, 55–59.

Smith, B. B. (1929). Judging the forecast for 1929. *Journal of the American Statistical Association*, **24**, 94–98.

Spanos, A. (1986). *Statistical Foundations of Econometric Modelling.* Cambridge: Cambridge University Press.

Tibshirani, R. (1996). Regression shrinkage and selection via the lasso. *Journal of the Royal Statistical Society B*, **58**, 267–288.

Yule, G. U. (1897). On the theory of correlation. *Journal of the Royal Statistical Society*, **60**, 812–838.

Yule, G. U. (1926). Why do we sometimes get nonsense-correlations between time-series? A study in sampling and the nature of time series (with discussion). *Journal of the Royal Statistical Society*, **89**, 1–64. Reprinted in Hendry, D. F., and Morgan, M. S. (1995), *The Foundations of Econometric Analysis*. Cambridge: Cambridge University Press.

3
Why Is the World Always Changing?

Abstract Empirical models used in disciplines as diverse as economics through to climatology analyze data assuming observations are from stationary processes even though the means and variances of most 'real world' time series change. We discuss some key sources of non-stationarity in demography, economics, politics and the environment, noting that (say) non-stationarity in economic data will 'infect' variables that are influenced by economics. Theory derivations, empirical models, forecasts and policy will go awry if the two forms of non-stationarity introduced above are not tackled. We illustrate non-stationary time series in a range of disciplines and discuss how to address the important difficulties that non-stationarity creates, as well as some potential benefits.

Keywords Sources of change · Wages, prices and productivity · Modelling non-stationarity

Many empirical models used in research and to guide policy in disciplines as diverse as economics to climate change analyze data by methods that assume observations come from stationary processes. However, most 'real

J. L. Castle and D. F. Hendry, *Modelling our Changing World*,
Palgrave Texts in Econometrics, https://doi.org/10.1007/978-3-030-21432-6_3

world' time series are not stationary in that the means and variances of outcomes change over time. Present levels of knowledge, living standards, average age of death etc., are not highly unlikely draws from their distributions in medieval times, but come from distributions with very different means and variances. For example, the average age of death in London in the 1860s was around 45, whereas today it is closer to 80—a huge change in the mean. Moreover, some individuals in the 1860s lived twice the average, namely into their 90s, whereas today, no one lives twice the average age, so the relative variance has also changed.

3.1 Major Sources of Changes

As well as the two World Wars causing huge disruption, loss of life, and massive damage to infrastructure, there have been numerous smaller conflicts, which are still devastating for those caught up in such conflict. In addition to those dramatic shifts noted above as causes of structural breaks, we could also include for the UK the post World War I crash; the 1926 general strike; and the creation of the European Union with the UK joining the EU (but now threatening to leave). There were many policy regime shifts, including periods on then off the Gold Standard; the Bretton Woods agreement in 1945; floating exchange rates from 1973; in and out of the Exchange Rate Mechanism (ERM) till October 1992; Keynesian fiscal policies; then Monetarist; followed by inflation targeting policies; and the start of the Euro zone. All that against a background of numerous important and evolving changes: globalization and development worldwide with huge increases in living standards and reductions in extreme poverty; changes in inequality, demography, health, longevity, and migration; legal reforms and different social mores; huge technology advances in electricity, refrigeration, transport, communications (including telephones, radio, television, and now mobiles), flight, nuclear power, medicine, new materials, computers, and containerization, with major industrial decline from cotton, coal, steel, and shipbuilding industries virtually vanishing, but being replaced by businesses based on new technologies and services.

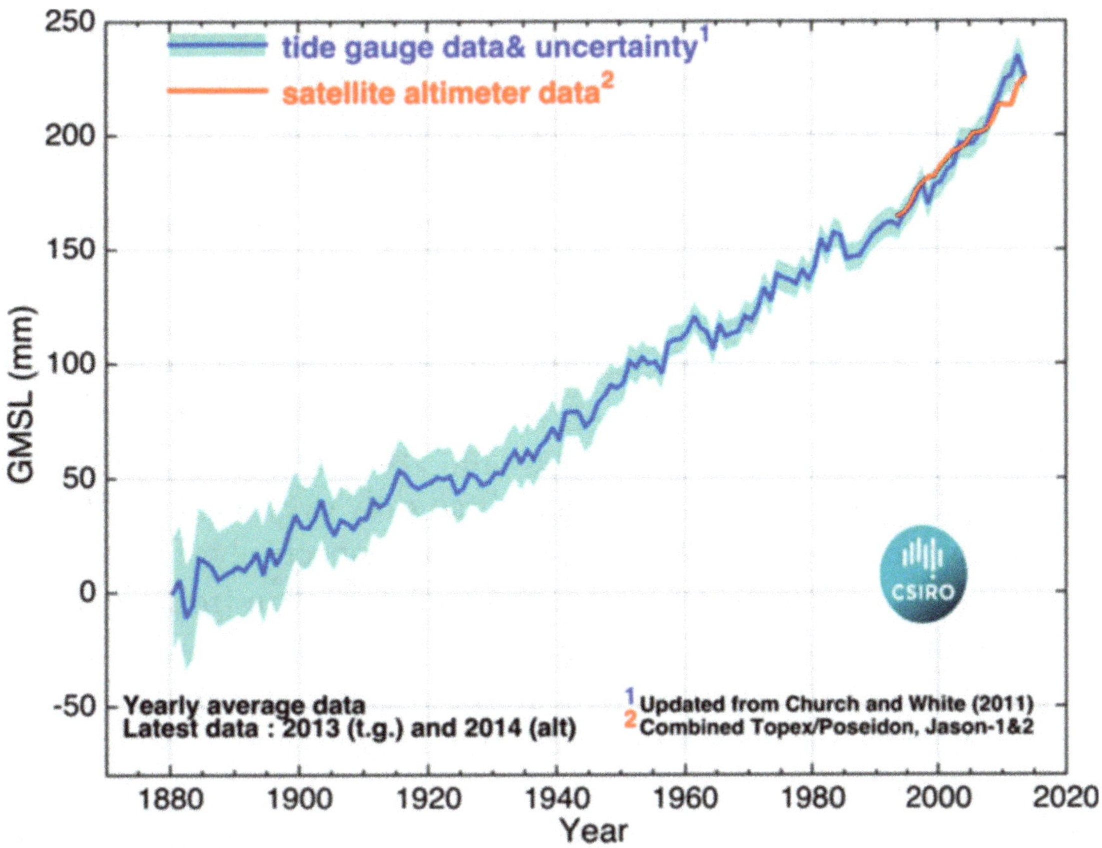

Fig. 3.1 Global mean sea-level (GMSL) has risen by more than 20 cm since 1880 (*Source* CSIRO)

Because economic data are non-stationary, that will 'infect' other variables which are influenced by economics (e.g., CO_2 emissions), and so spread like a pandemic to most socio-economic and related variables, and probably will feed back onto economics. Many theories, most empirical models of time series, and all forecasts will go awry when both forms of non-stationarity introduced above are not tackled. A key feature of processes where the distributions of outcomes shift over time is that probabilities of events calculated in one time period need not apply in another: 'once in a hundred years' can become 'once a decade'. Flooding by storm surges becomes more likely with sea-levels rising from climate change. Figure 3.1 shows that global mean sea-level has risen over 20 cm since 1880, and is now rising at 3.4 mm p.a. versus 1.3 mm p.a. over 1850–1992 (see e.g., Jevrejeva et al. 2016).[1]

[1] See https://www.cmar.csiro.au/sealevel/sl_data_cmar.html.

More generally, an important source of changes are environmental, perhaps precipitated by social and economic behaviour like CO_2 emissions and their consequences, but also occurring naturally as with earthquakes, volcanic eruptions and phenomena like El Niño. Policy decisions have to take non-stationarities into account: as another obvious example, with increasing longevity, pension payments and life insurance commitments and contracts are affected.

We first provide more illustrations of non-stationary time series to emphasize how dramatically many have changed. Figure 3.2, left-hand panel graphs UK annual nominal wages and prices over the long historical period 1860–2014. These have changed radically over the last 150 years, rising by more than **70,000%** and **10,000%** respectively. Their rates of growth have also changed intermittently, as can be seen from the changing slopes of the graph lines. The magnitude of a 25% change is marked to clarify the scale. It is hard to imagine any 'revamping' of the statistical assumptions such that these outcomes could be construed as coming from stationary processes.[2]

Figure 3.2, right-hand panel, records productivity, measured as output per person per year, with real wages (i.e., in constant prices), namely the difference between the two (log) time series in the left-hand panel. Both trend strongly, but move closely together, albeit with distinct slope changes and 'bumps' en route. The 'flat-lining' after the 'Great Recession' of 2008–2012 is highlighted by the ellipse. The wider 25% change marker highlights the reduced scale. Nevertheless, both productivity and real wages have increased by about sevenfold over the period, a huge rise in living standards. This reflects a second key group of causes of the changing world: increased knowledge inducing technical and medical progress, embodied in the latest vintage of capital equipment used by an increasingly educated workforce.

Figure 3.3(a) plots annual wage inflation (price inflation is similar as Fig. 2.4(b) showed) to emphasize that changes, or growth rates, also can be non-stationary, here from both major shifts in means (the thicker black line in Panel (a)), as well as in variances. Compare the quiescent 50-year

[2]It is sometimes argued that economic time series could be stationary around a deterministic trend, but it seems unlikely that GDP would continue trending upwards if nobody worked.

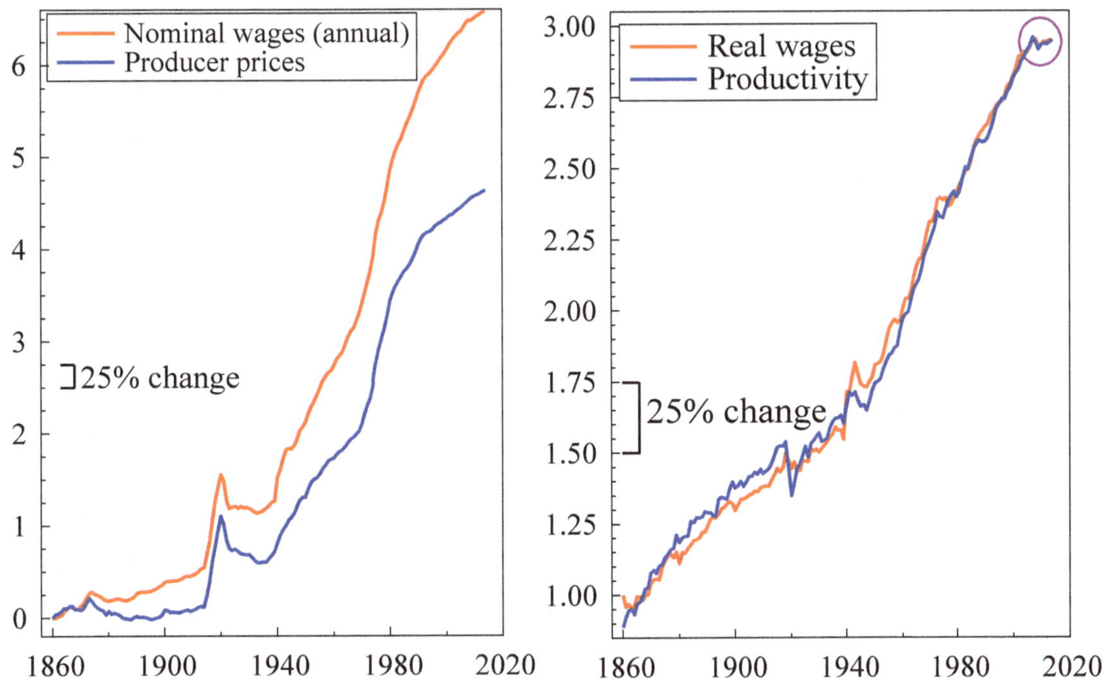

Fig. 3.2 Indexes of UK wages and prices (left-hand panel) and UK real wages and productivity (right-hand panel), both on log scales

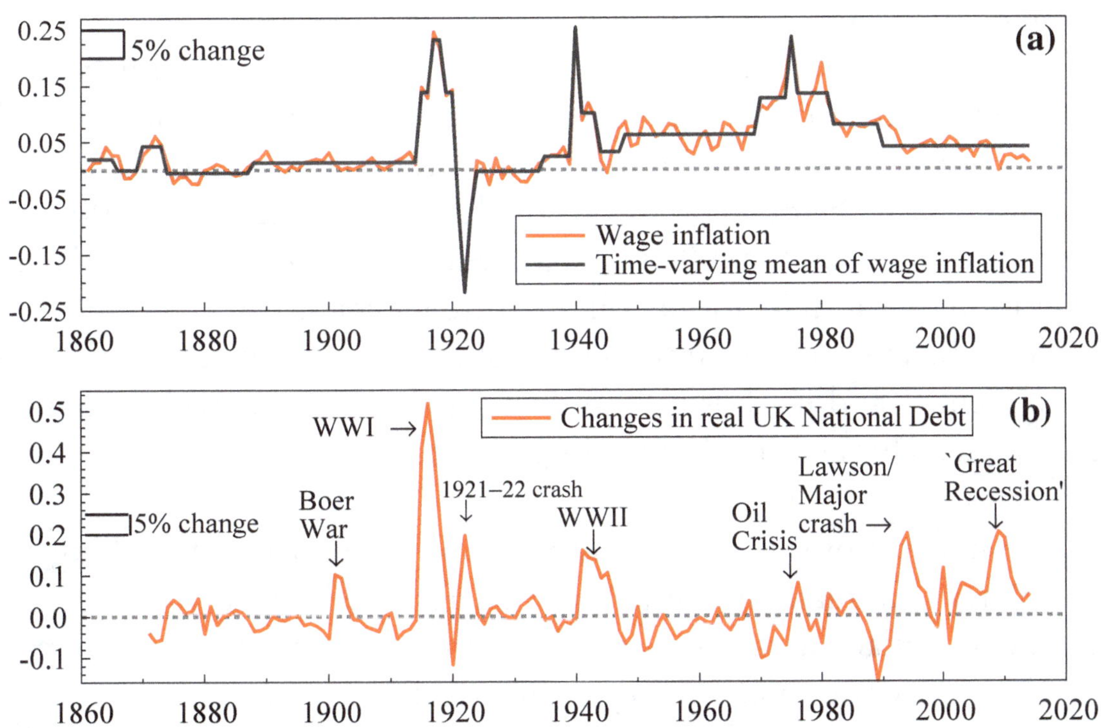

Fig. 3.3 (**a**) UK wage inflation; and (**b**) changes in real national debt with major historical events shown

period before 1914 with the following 50 years, noting the scale of 5% in (a). Historically, wages have fallen (and risen) more than 20% in a year.

Figure 3.3(b) records changes in real UK National Debt, with the associated events. In any empirical, observationally-based discipline, 'causes' can never be 'proved', merely attributed as overwhelmingly likely. The events shown on Fig. 3.3(b) nevertheless seem to be the proximate causes: real National Debt rises sharply in crises, including wars and major recessions. Even in constant prices, National Debt has on occasion risen by 50% in a year—and that despite inflation then being above 20%—although here the 5% scale is somewhat narrower than in (a). Wars and major recessions are the third set of reasons why the world is ever changing, although at a deeper level of explanation one might seek to understand their causes.

None of the above real-world time series has a constant mean or variance, so cannot be stationary. The two distinct features of stochastic trends and sudden shifts are exhibited, namely 'wandering' widely, most apparent in Fig. 3.2, and suddenly shifting as in Fig. 3.3, features that will recur. Such phenomena are not limited to economic data, but were seen above in demographic and climatological time series.

Figure 3.4 illustrates the non-stationary nature of recent climate time series compared to ice-age cycles for global concentrations of atmospheric CO_2 relative to recent rapid annual increases (see e.g., Sundquist and Keeling 2009). The observations in the left-hand panel are at 1000 year intervals, over almost 800,000 years, whereas those in the right-hand panel are monthly, so at dramatically different frequencies.

Given the almost universal absence of stationarity in real-world time series, Hendry and Juselius (2000) delineated four issues with important consequences for empirical modelling, restated here as:

(A) the key role of stationarity assumptions in empirical modelling and inference in many studies, despite its absence in data;
(B) the potentially hazardous impacts on theory analyses, empirical modelling, forecasting and policy of incorrectly assuming stationarity;
(C) the many sources of the two main forms of non-stationarity (evolution and abrupt shifts), that need to be considered when modelling;
(D) yet fortunately, statistical analyses can often be undertaken to eliminate many of the most adverse effects of non-stationarity.

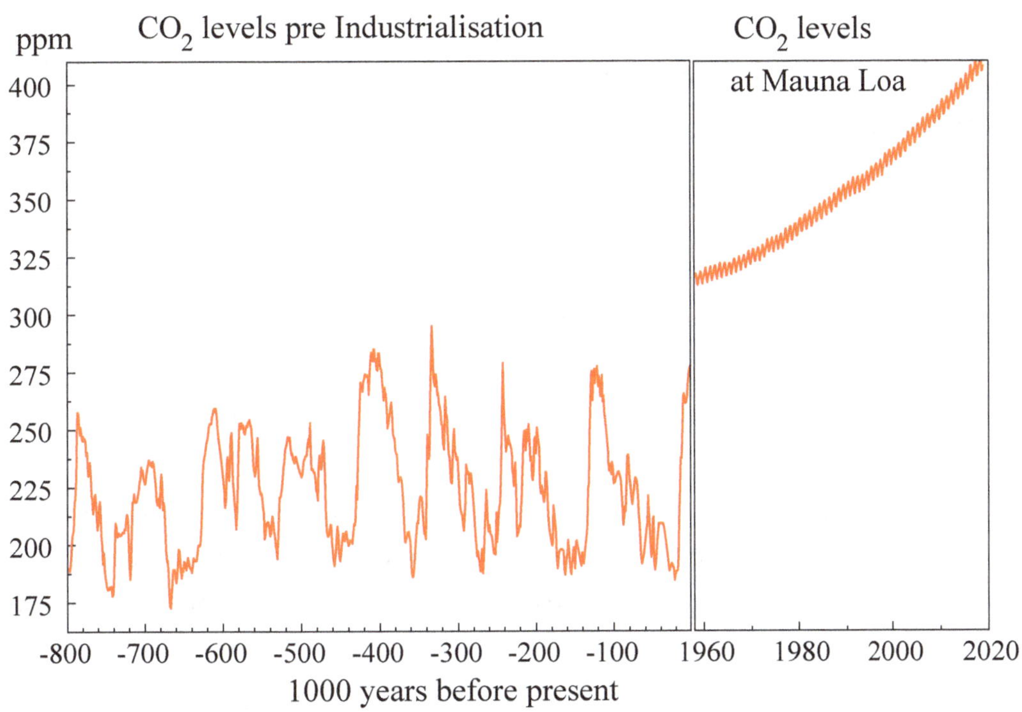

Fig. 3.4 Levels of atmospheric CO_2 in parts per million (ppm)

We now consider issues (A), (B) and (D) in turn: the sources referred to in (C) have been discussed immediately above.

3.2 Problems if Incorrectly Modelling Non-stationarity

(A) Theories and models of human behaviour that assume stationarity, so do not account for the non-stationarity in their data, will continually fail to explain outcomes. In a stationary world, the best predictor of what we expect an event to be like tomorrow should be based on all the information available today. This is the conditional expectation given all the relevant information. In elementary econometrics and statistics textbooks, such a conditional expectation is proved to provide the smallest variance of all unbiased predictors of the mean of the distribution. An implicit, and never stated, assumption is that the distributions over which such conditional expectations are calculated are constant over time. But if the mean of its distribution shifts, a conditional expectation today can predict a value that is far from tomorrow's outcome. This will create a 'disequilibrium', where individuals who formed such expectations will need to adjust to their mistakes.

(B) In fact, the mathematical basis of much of 'modern' macroeconomics requires stationarity to be valid, and fails when distributions shift in unanticipated ways. As an analogy, continuing to use such mathematical tools in non-stationary worlds is akin to insisting on using Euclidian geometry to measure angles of triangles on a globe: then navigation can go seriously adrift. We return to this aspect in the next chapter.

In turn, the accuracy and precision of forecasts are affected by non-stationarity. Its presence leads to far larger interval forecasts (the range within which a forecaster anticipates the future values should lie) than would occur in stationary processes, so if a stationary model is incorrectly fitted, its calculated uncertainty can dramatically under-estimate the true uncertainty. This is part of the explanation for the nonsense-regressions issue we noted above. Worse still, unexpected location shifts usually lead to forecast failure, where forecast errors are systematically much larger than would be expected in the absence of shifts, as happened during the Financial Crisis and Great Recession over 2008–2012. Consequently, the uncertainty of forecasts can be much greater than that calculated from past data, both because the sources of evolution in data cumulate over time, and also because 'unknown unknowns' can occur, especially unanticipated location shifts.

Scenarios based on outcomes produced by simulating empirical models are often used in economic policy, for example, by the Bank of England in deciding its interest-rate decisions. When the model is a poor representation of the non-stationarities prevalent in the economy, policy changes (such as interest-rate increases) can actually cause location shifts that then lead to forecast failure, so after the event, what had seemed a good decision is seen to be badly based.

Thus, all four arenas of theory, modelling, forecasting and policy face serious hazards from non-stationarity unless it is appropriately handled. Fortunately, in each setting some actions can be taken, albeit providing palliative, rather than complete, solutions. Concerning theory derivations, there is an urgent need to develop approaches that allow for economic agents always facing disequilibrium settings, and needing error-correction strategies after suffering unanticipated location shifts. Empirical modelling can detect and remove location shifts that have happened: for example, statistical tools for dealing with shifts enabled Statistics Norway to revise their economic forecasts within two weeks of the shock induced by the Lehmann Brothers bankruptcy in 2008. Modelling can also avoid the 'nonsense relation' problem by checking for genuine long-run connections between variables (called cointegration, the development of which led to a Nobel Prize for Sir Clive Granger), as well as embody feedbacks that help correct previous mistakes. Forecasting devices can allow for the ever-growing uncertainty arising from cumulating shocks. There are also methods for helping to robustify forecasts against systematic failure after unanticipated location shifts. Tests have been formulated to check for policy changes having caused location shifts in the available data, and if found, warn against the use of those models for making future policy decisions.

(D) Finally, although non-stationary time series data are harder to model and forecast, there are some important benefits deriving from non-stationarity. Long-run relationships are difficult to isolate with stationary data: since all connections between variables persist unchanged over time, it is not easy to determine genuine causal links. However, cumulated shocks help reveal what relationships stay together (i.e., cointegrate) for long time periods. This is even more true of location shifts, where only connected variables will move together after a shift (called co-breaking). Such shifts also alter the correlations between variables, facilitating more accurate estimates of empirical models, and revealing what variables are not consistently connected. Strong trends and location shifts can also highlight genuine connections, such as cointegration, through a fog of measurement errors in data series. Lastly, past location shifts allow the tests noted in the previous paragraph to be implemented before a wrong policy is adopted. The next chapter considers how to model trends and shifts and the potential benefits of doing so.

References

Hendry, D. F., and Juselius, K. (2000). Explaining cointegration analysis: Part I. *Energy Journal*, **21**, 1–42.

Jevrejeva, S., Jackson, L. P., Riva, R. E. M., Grinsted, A., and Moore, J. C. (2016). Coastal sea level rise with warming above 2°C. *Proceedings of the National Academy of Sciences*, **113(47)**, 13342–13347.

Sundquist, E. T., and Keeling, R. F. (2009). The Mauna Loa carbon dioxide record: Lessons for long-term earth observations. *Geophysical Monograph Series*, **183**, 27–35.

4

Making Trends and Breaks Work to Our Advantage

Abstract The previous Chapter noted there are benefits of non-stationarity, so we now consider that aspect in detail. Non-stationarity can be caused by stochastic trends and shifts of data distributions. The simplest example of the first is a random walk of the kind created by Yule, where the current observation equals the previous one perturbed by a random shock. This form of integrated process occurs in economics, demography and climatology. Combinations of I(1) processes are also usually I(1), but in some situations stochastic trends can cancel to an I(0) outcome, called cointegration. Distributions can shift in many ways, but location shifts are the most pernicious forms for theory, empirical modelling, forecasting and policy. We discuss how they too can be handled, with the potential benefit of highlighting when variables are not related as assumed.

Keywords Integrated processes · Serial correlation · Stochastic trends · Cointegration · Location shifts · Co-breaking · Dynamic stochastic general equilibrium models (DSGEs)

J. L. Castle and D. F. Hendry, *Modelling our Changing World*,
Palgrave Texts in Econometrics, https://doi.org/10.1007/978-3-030-21432-6_4

4.1 Potential Solutions to Stochastic Trend Non-stationarity

As described in Sect. 2.2, Yule created integrated processes deliberately, but there are many economic, social and natural mechanisms that induce integratedness in data. Perhaps the best known example of an I(1) process is a random walk, where the current value is equal to the previous value plus a random error. Thus the change in a random walk is just a random error. Such a process can wander widely, and was first proposed by Bachelier (1900) to describe the behaviour of prices in speculative markets. However, such processes also occur in demography (see Lee and Carter 1992) as well as economics, because the stock of a variable, like population or inventories, cumulates the net inflow as discussed for Fig. 2.3. A natural integrated process is the concentration of atmospheric CO_2, as emissions cumulate due to CO_2's long atmospheric lifetime, as in the right-hand panel of Fig. 3.4. Such emissions have been mainly anthropogenic since the industrial revolution. When the inflows to an integrated process are random, the variance will grow over time by cumulating past perturbations, violating stationarity. Thus, unlike an I(0) process which varies around a constant mean with a constant variance, an I(1) process has an increasing variance, usually called a stochastic trend, and may also 'drift' in a general direction over time to induce a trend in the level.

Cumulating past random shocks should make the resulting time series relatively smooth since successive observations share a large number of past inputs. Also the correlations between successive values will be high, and only decline slowly as their distance apart increases–the persistence discussed in Sect. 2.1. Figure 4.1(a), (b) illustrates for the logs of wages and real wages, where the sequence of successive correlations shown is called a correlogram. Taking wages in the top-left panel (a) as an example, the outcome in any year is still correlated 0.97 with the outcome 20 years previously, and similar high correlations between variables 20 years apart hold for real wages. Values outside the dashed lines are significantly different from zero at 5%.

Differencing is the opposite of integration, so an I(1) process has first differences that are I(0). Thus, despite its non-stationarity, an I(1) process can be reduced to I(0) by differencing, an idea that underlies the

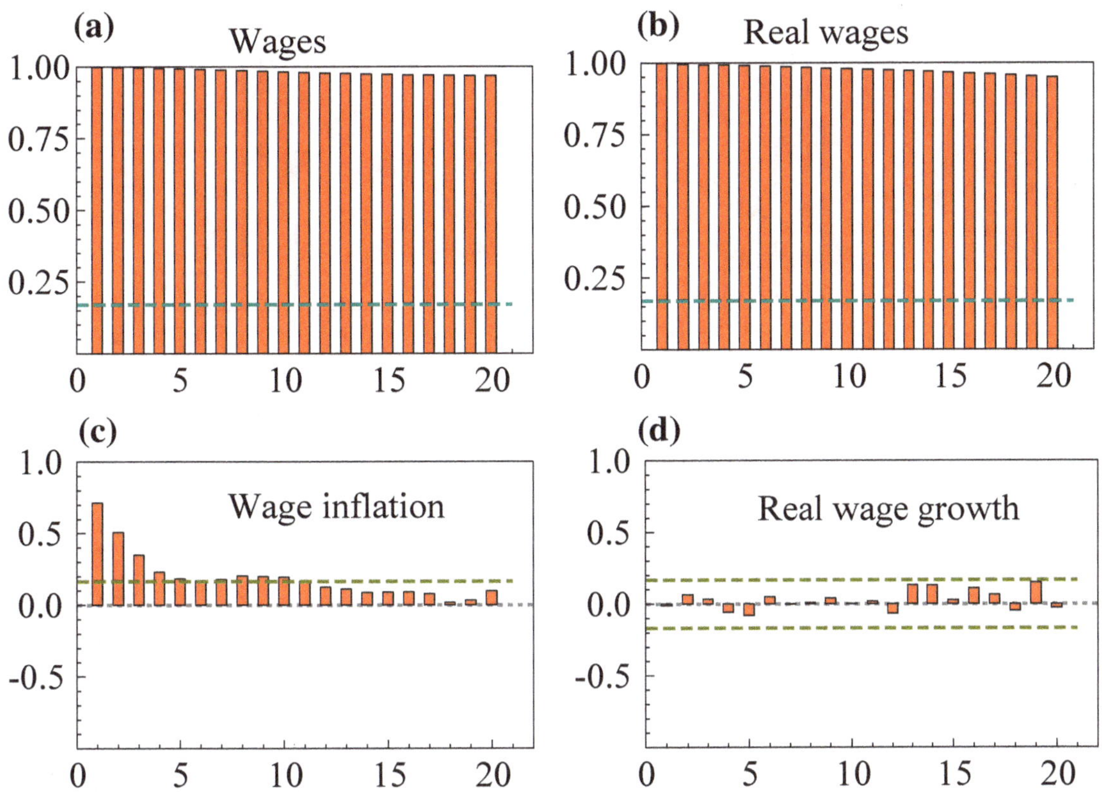

Fig. 4.1 Twenty successive serial correlations for **(a)** nominal wages; **(b)** real wages; **(c)** wage inflation; and **(d)** real wage growth

empirical modelling and forecasting approach in Box and Jenkins (1976). Now successive values in the correlogram should decline quite quickly, as Figs. 4.1(c) and (d) show for the differences of these two time series. Wage inflation is quite highly correlated with its values one and two periods earlier, but there are much smaller correlations further back, although even as far back as 20 years, all the correlations are positive. However, the growth of real wages seems essentially random in terms of its correlogram. As a warning, such evidence does not imply that real wage growth cannot be modelled empirically, merely that the preceeding value by itself does not explain the current outcome.

Differences of I(1) time series should also be approximately Normally distributed when the shocks are nearly Normal. Such outcomes implicitly suppose there are no additional 'abnormal' shocks such as location shifts. Figure 4.2 illustrates for wage and price inflation, and the growth in real wages and productivity. None of the four distributions is Normal, with all

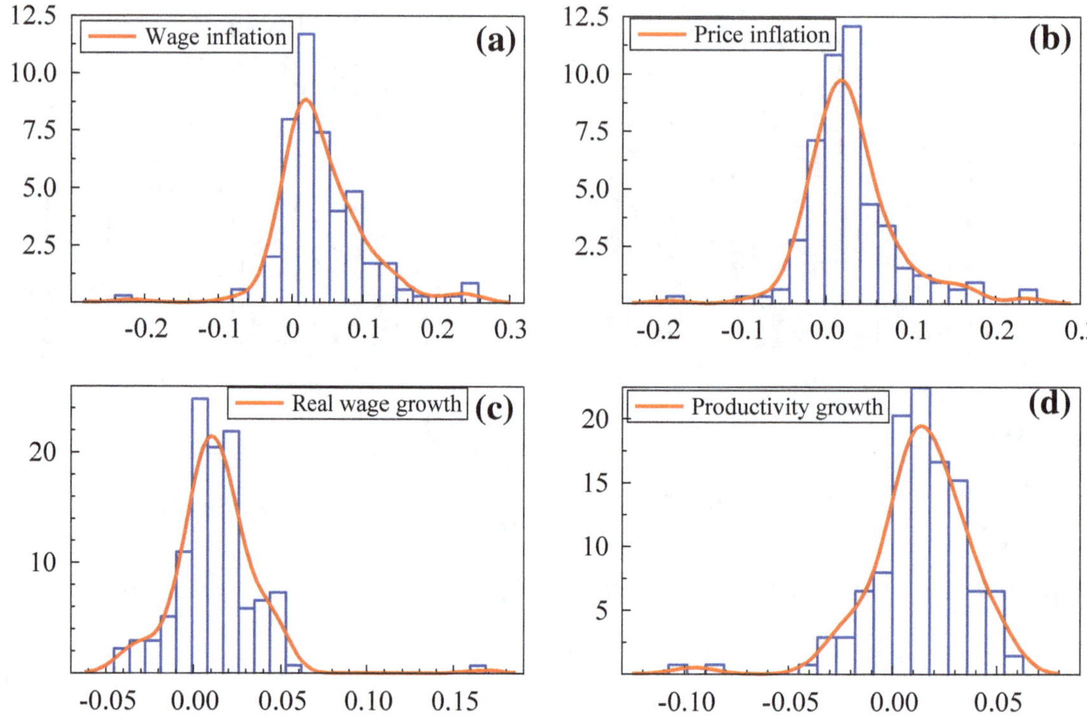

Fig. 4.2 Densities of the differences for: (**a**) nominal wages; (**b**) prices; (**c**) real wages and (**d**) productivity

revealing large outliers, which cannot be a surprise given their time series graphs in Fig. 3.2.

To summarise, both the mean and the variance of I(1) processes change over time, and successive values are highly interdependent. As Yule (1926) showed, this can lead to nonsense regression problems. Moreover, the conventional forms of distributions assumed for estimates of parameters in empirical models under stationarity no longer hold, so statistical inference becomes hazardous unless the non-stationarity is taken into account.

4.2 Cointegration Between I(1) Processes

Linear combinations of several I(1) processes are usually I(1) as well. However, stochastic trends can cancel between series to yield an I(0) outcome. This is called cointegration. Cointegrated relationships define a 'long-run equilibrium trajectory', departures from which induce 'equilibrium correc-

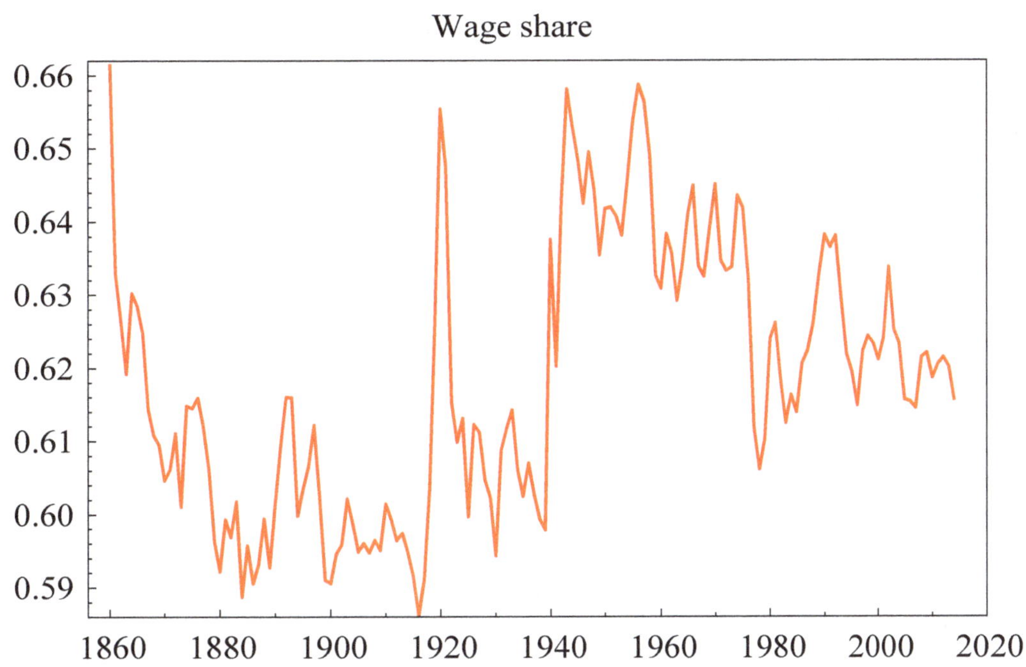

Fig. 4.3 Time series for the wage share

tion' that moves the relevant system back towards that path.[1] Equilibrium-correction mechanisms are a very large class of models that coincide with cointegrated relations when data are I(1), but also apply to I(0) processes which are implicitly always cointegrated in that all linear combinations are I(0). When the data are I(2) there is a generalized form of cointegration leading to I(0) combinations. Equilibrium-correction mechanisms (EqCMs) can be written in a representation in which changes in variables are inter-related, but also include lagged values of the I(0) combinations. EqCMs have the key property that they converge back to the long-run equilibrium of the data being modelled. This is invaluable when that equilibrium is constant, but as we will see, can be problematic if there are shifts in equilibria.

Real wages and productivity, shown in Fig. 3.2, are each I(1), but their differential, which is the wage share shown in Fig. 4.3, could be I(0). The wage share cancels the separate stochastic trends in real wages and productivity to create a possible cointegrating relation where the stochastic

[1]Davidson et al. (1978), and much of the subsequent literature, call these 'error correction'.

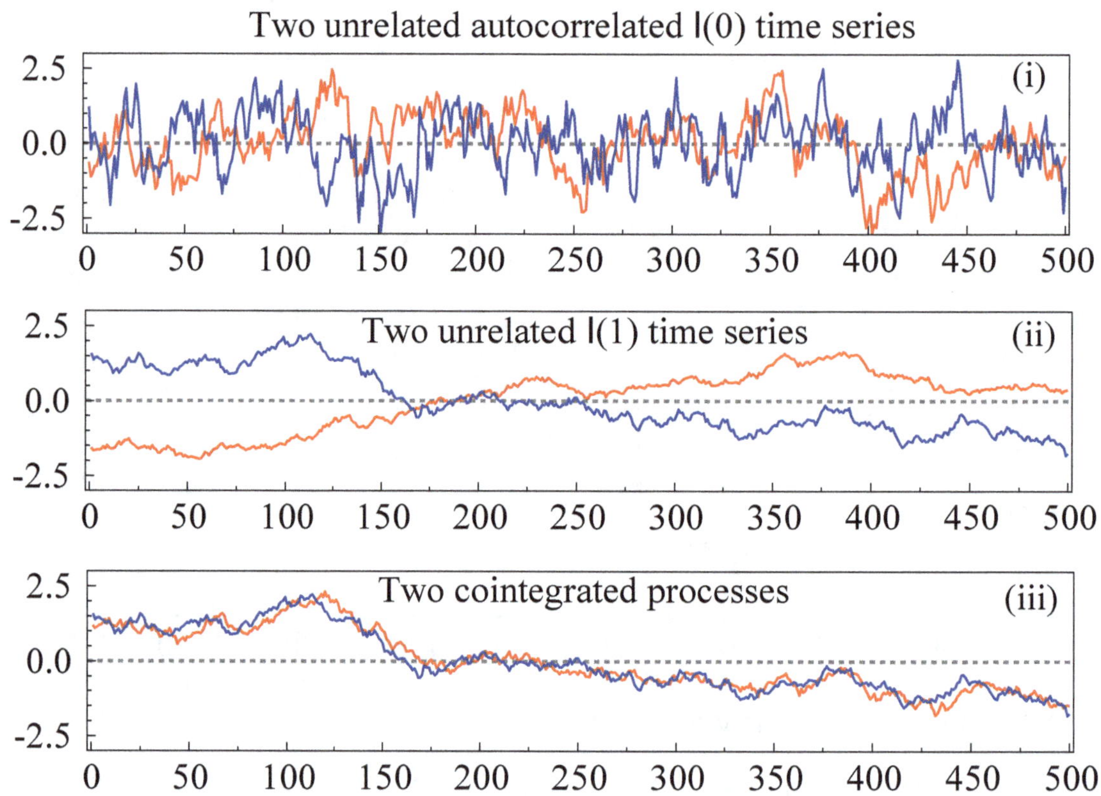

Fig. 4.4 Pairs of artificial time series: (i) unrelated I(0); (ii) unrelated I(1); (iii) cointegrated

trends have been removed, but there also seem to be long swings and perhaps location shifts, an issue we consider in Sect. 4.3.

To illustrate pairs of variables that are (i) unrelated I(0) but autocorrelated, (ii) unrelated I(1), and (iii) cointegrated, Fig. 4.4 shows 500 observations on computer-generated data. The very different behaviours are marked, and although rarely so obvious in practice, the close trajectories of real wages and productivity in Fig. 3.3 over 150 years resembles the bottom panel.

In economics, integrated-cointegrated data seem almost inevitable because of the Granger (1981) Representation Theorem, for which he received the Sveriges Riksbank Prize in Economic Science in Memory of Alfred Nobel in 2003. His result shows that cointegration between variables must occur if there are fewer decision variables (e.g., your income and bank account balance) than the number of decisions (e.g., hundreds of shopping items: see Hendry 2004, for an explanation). If that setting was the only source of non-stationarity, there would be two ways of bringing an analysis involving integrated processes back to I(0): differencing to remove cumulative inputs (which always achieves that aim), or finding linear combinations that form cointegrating relations. There must always be fewer cointegrating relations than the total number of variables, as otherwise the system would be stationary, so some variables must still be differenced to represent the entire system as I(0).

Cointegration is not exclusive to economic time series. The radiative forcing of greenhouse gases and other variables affecting global climate cointegrate with surface temperatures, consistent with models from physics (see Kaufmann et al. 2013; Pretis 2019). Thus, cointegration occurs naturally, and is consistent with many existing theories in the natural sciences where interacting systems of differential equations in non-stationary time series can be written as a cointegrating model.

Other sources of non-stationarity also matter, however, especially shifts in the means of data distributions of I(0) variables, including equilibrium correction means, and growth rate averages, so we turn to this second main source of non-stationarity. There is a tendency in the econometrics literature to identify 'non-stationarity' purely with integrated data (time series with unit roots), and so incorrectly claim that differencing a time series induces stationarity. Certainly, a unit root is removed by considering the difference, but there are other sources of non-stationarity, so for clarity we refer to the general case as wide-sense non-stationarity.

4.3 Location Shifts

Location shifts are changes from the previous mean of an I(0) variable. There have been enormous historical changes since 1860 in hours of work, real incomes, disease prevalence, sanitation, infant mortality, and average age of death among many other facets of life: see http://ourworldindata.org/ for comprehensive coverage. Figure 3.2 showed how greatly log wages and prices had increased over 1860–2014 with real wages rising sevenfold. Such huge increases could not have been envisaged in 1860. Uncertainty abounds, both in the real world and in our knowledge thereof. However, some events are so uncertain that probabilities of their happening cannot be sensibly assigned. We call such irreducible uncertainty 'extrinsic unpredictability', corresponding to unknown unknowns: see Hendry and Mizon (2014). A pernicious form of extrinsic unpredictability affecting inter-temporal analyses, empirical modelling, forecasting and policy interventions is that of unanticipated location shifts, namely shifts that occur at unanticipated times, changing by unexpected magnitudes and directions.

Figure 4.5 illustrates a hypothetical setting. The initial distribution is either a standard Normal (solid line) with mean zero and variance unity, or a 'fat-tailed' distribution (dashed line), which has a high probability of generating 'outliers' at unknown times and of unknown magnitudes and signs (sometimes called anomalous 'black swan events' as in Taleb 2007). As I(1) time series can be transformed back to I(0) by differencing or cointegration, the Normal distribution often remains the basis for calculating probabilities for statistical inference, as in random sampling from a known distribution. Hendry and Mizon (2014) call this 'intrinsic unpredictability', because the uncertainty in the outcome is intrinsic to the properties of the random variables. Large outliers provide examples of 'instance unpredictability' since their timings, magnitudes and signs are uncertain, even when they are expected to occur in general, as in speculative asset markets.

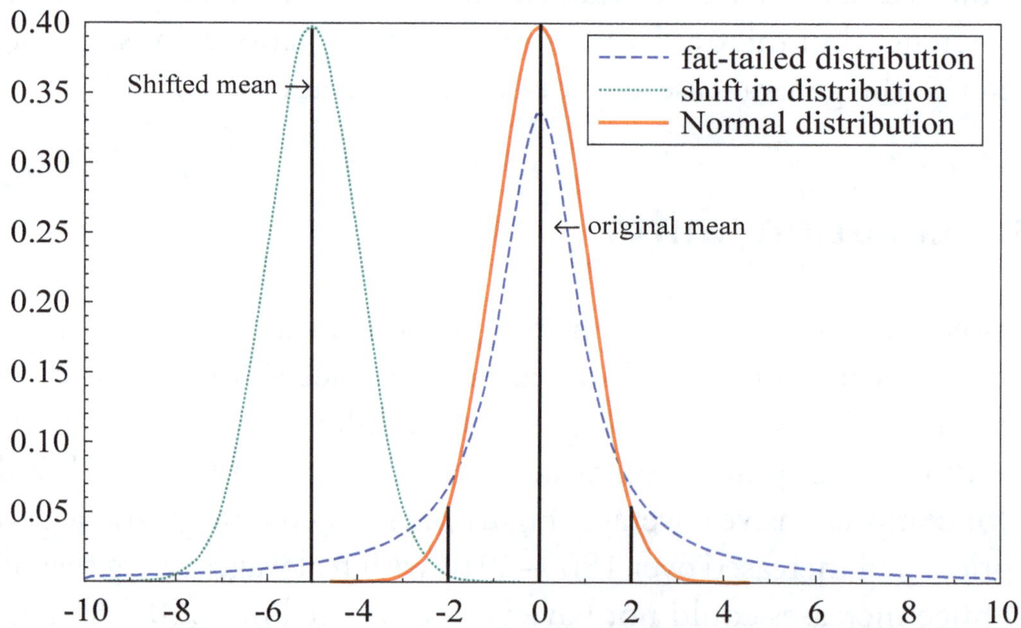

Fig. 4.5 Location shift in a normal or a fat-tailed distribution

However, in Fig. 4.5 the baseline distribution experiences a location shift to a new Normal distribution (dotted line) with a mean of −5. As we have already seen, there are many causes for such shifts, and many shifts have occurred historically, precipitated by changes in legislation, wars, financial innovation, science and technology, medical advances, climate change, social mores, evolving beliefs, and different political and economic regimes. Extrinsically unpredictable location shifts can make the new ordinary seem highly unusual relative to the past. In Fig. 4.5, after the shift, outcomes will now usually lie between 3 and 7 standard deviations away from the *previous* mean, generating an apparent 'flock' of black swans, which could never happen with independent sampling from the baseline distribution, even when fat-tails are possible. During the Financial Crisis in 2008, the possibility of location shifts generating many extremely unlikely bad draws does not seem to have been included in risk models. But extrinsic unpredictability happens in the real world (see e.g., Soros 2008): as we have remarked, current outcomes are not highly discrepant draws from the distributions prevalent in the Middle Ages, but 'normal' draws from present distributions that have shifted greatly. Moreover, the distributions of many data differences are not stationary: for example, real growth per capita in the UK has increased intermittently since the Industrial Revolution as seen in Fig. 3.2, and most nominal differences have experienced location shifts, illustrated by Fig. 3.3. Hendry (2015) provides dozens of other examples.

4.4 Dynamic-Stochastic General Equilibrium (DSGE) Models

Everyone has to take decisions at some point in time that will affect their future in important ways: marrying, purchasing a house with a mortgage, making an investment in a risky asset, starting a pension or life insurance, and so on. The information available at the time reflects the past and present but obviously does not include knowledge of the future. Consequently, a view has to be taken about possible futures that might affect the outcomes.

All too often, such views are predicated on there being no unanticipated future changes relevant to that decision, namely the environment is assumed to be relatively stationary. Certainly, there are periods of reasonable stability when observing how past events unfolded can assist in planning for the future. But as this book has stressed, unexpected events occur, especially unpredicted shifts in the distributions of relevant variables at unanticipated times. Hendry and Mizon (2014) show that the intermittent occurrence of 'extrinsic unpredictability' has dramatic consequences for any theory analyses of time-dependent behaviour, empirical modelling of time series, forecasting, and policy interventions. In particular, the mathematical basis of the class of models widely used by central banks, namely DSGE models, ceases to be valid as DSGEs are based on an inter-temporal optimization calculus that requires the absence of distributional shifts.

This is not an 'academic' critique: the supposedly 'structural' Bank of England Quarterly Model (BEQM) broke down during the Financial Crisis, and has since been replaced by another DSGE called COMPASS, which may be pointing in the wrong direction: see Hendry and Muellbauer (2018).

DSGE Models

Many of the theoretical equations in DSGE models take a form in which a variable today, denoted y_t, depends on its 'expected future value' often written as $\mathsf{E}_t[y_{t+1}|\mathcal{I}_t]$, where $\mathsf{E}_t[\cdot]$ indicates the date at which the expectation is formed about the variable in the [ ]. Such expectations are conditional on what information is available, which we denoted by $\mathcal{I}_t$, so are naturally called conditional expectations, and are defined to be the average over the relevant conditional distribution. If the relation between y_{t+1} and $\mathcal{I}_t$ shifts as in Fig. 4.5, y_{t+1} could be far from what was expected.

As we noted above, in a stationary world, a 'classic' proof in elementary statistics courses is that the conditional expectation has the smallest variance of all unbiased predictors of the mean of their distribution. By basing their expectations for tomorrow on today's distribution, DSGE formulations assume stationarity, possibly after 'removing' stochastic trends by some method of de-trending. From Fig. 4.5 it is rather obvious that the previous mean, and hence the previous conditional expectation, is not an unbiased predictor of the outcome after a location shift.

As we have emphasized, underlying distributions can and do shift unexpectedly. Of course, we are all affected to some extent by unanticipated shifts of the distributions relevant to our lives, such as unexpectedly being made redundant, sudden increases in mortgage costs or tax rates, or reduced pension values after a stock market crash. However, we then usually change our plans, and perhaps also our views of the future. The first unfortunate outcome for DSGE models is that their parameters shift after a location shift. The second is that their mathematical derivations usually assume that the agents in their model do not change their behaviour from what would be the optimum in a stationary world. However, as ordinary people seem unlikely to be better at forecasting breaks than professional economists, or even quickly learning their implications after they have occurred, most of us are forced to adapt our plans after such shifts.

By ignoring the possibility of distributional shifts, conditional expectations can certainly be 'proved' to be unbiased, but that does not imply they will be in practice. Some econometric models of inflation, such as the so-called new-Keynesian Phillips curve, involve expectations of the unknown future value written as $\mathsf{E}[y_{t+1}|\mathcal{I}_t]$. A common procedure is to replace that conditional expectation by the actual future outcome y_{t+1}, arguing that the conditional expectation is unbiased for the actual outcome, so will only differ from it by unpredictable random shocks with a mean of zero. That implication only holds if there have been no shifts in the distributions of the variables, and otherwise will entail mis-specified empirical models that can seriously mislead in their policy implications as Castle et al. (2014) demonstrate.

There is an intimate link between forecast failure, the biasedness of conditional expectations and the inappropriate application of inter-temporal optimization analysis: when the first is due to an unanticipated location shift, the other two follow. Worse, a key statistical theorem in modern macroeconomics, called the law of iterated expectations, no longer holds when the distributions from which conditional expectations are formed change over time. The law of iterated expectations implies that today's expectation of tomorrow's outcome, given what we know today, is equal to tomorrow's expectation. Thus, one can 'iterate' expectations over time.

The theorem is not too hard to prove when all the distributions involved are the same, but it need not hold when any of the distributions shift between today and tomorrow for exactly the same reasons as Fig. 2.8 reveals: that shift entails forecast failure, a violation of today's expectation being unbiased for tomorrow, and the failure of the law of iterated expectations.

As a consequence, dynamic stochastic general equilibrium models are inherently non-structural; their mathematical basis fails when substantive distributional shifts occur and their parameters will be changed. This adverse property of all DSGEs explains the 'break down' of BEQM facing the Financial Crisis and Great Recession as many distributions shifted markedly, including that of interest rates (to unprecedently low levels from Quantitative Easing) and consequently the distributions of endowments across individuals and families. Unanticipated changes in underlying probability distributions, especially location shifts, have detrimental impacts on all economic analyses involving conditional expectations and hence intertemporal derivations as well as causing forecast failure. What we now show is that with appropriate tools, the impacts of outliers and location shifts on empirical modelling can be taken into account.

4.5 Handling Location Shifts

At first sight, location shifts seem highly problematic for econometric modelling, but as with stochastic trends, there are several potential solutions. Differencing a time series will also inadvertently convert a location shift to an impulse (an impulse in the first difference is equivalent to a step-shift in the level). Secondly, time series can co-break, analogous to cointegration, in that location shifts can cancel between series.

Thus, time series can be combined to remove some or all of the individual shifts. Individual series may exhibit multiple shifts, but when modelling one series by another, co-breaking implies that fewer shifts will be detected when the series break together. Figure 3.2 showed the divergent strong but changing trends in nominal wages and prices, and Fig. 3.3 recorded the many shifts in wage inflation. Nevertheless, as shown by the time series of real wage growth in Fig. 4.6, almost all the shifts in wage inflation and price inflation cancelled over 1860–2014. The only one not

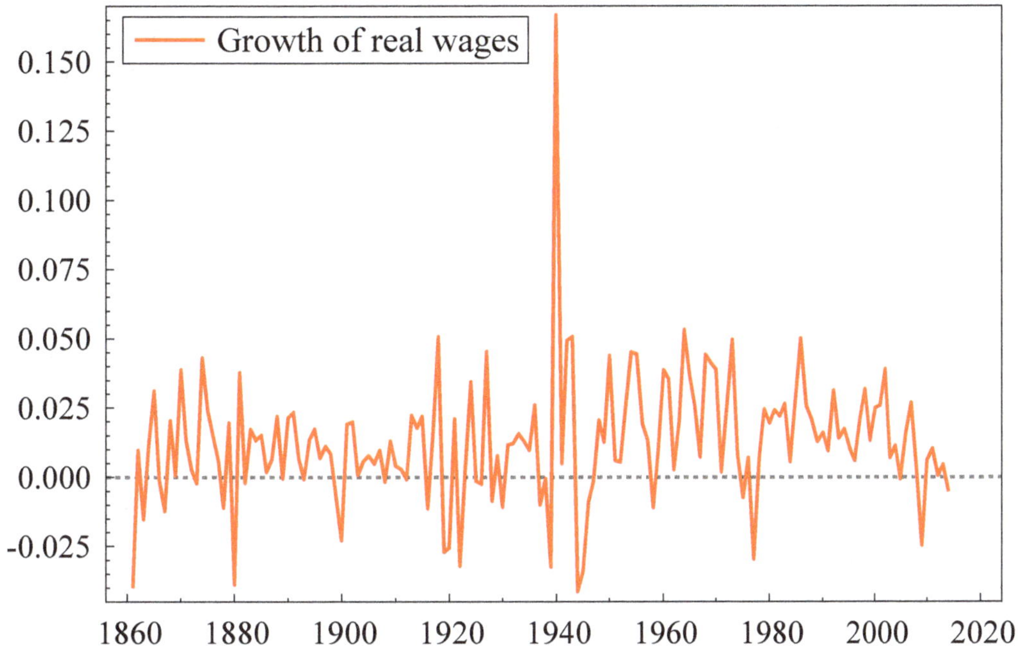

Fig. 4.6 Partial co-breaking between wage and price inflation

to is the huge 'spike' in 1940, which was a key step in the UK's war effort, to encourage new workers to replace army recruits.

The third possible solution is to find all the location shifts and outliers whatever their magnitudes and signs then include indicators for them in the model. To do so requires us to solve the apparently impossible problem of selecting from more candidate variables in a model than observations. Hendry (1999) accidently stumbled over a solution. Most contributors to Magnus and Morgan (1999) had found that models of US real per capita annual food demand were non-constant over the sample 1929–1952, so dropped that earlier data from their empirical modelling. Figure 2.4(a) indeed suggests very different behaviour pre and post 1952, but by itself that does not entail that econometric models which include explanatory variables like food prices and real incomes must shift. To investigate why, yet replicate others' models, Hendry added impulse indicators (which are 'dummy variables' that are zero everywhere except for unity at one data point) for all observations pre-1952, which revealed three large outliers corresponding to a US Great Depression food programme and post-war de-rationing. To check that his model was constant from 1953 onwards, he later added impulse indicators for that period, thereby including more variables plus indicators than observations, but only entered in his model in two large blocks, each much smaller than the number of observations. This has led to a statistical theory for modelling multiple outliers and location shifts (see e.g., Johansen and Nielsen 2009; Castle et al. 2015), available in our computational tool *Autometrics* (Doornik 2009) and in the package *Gets* (Pretis et al. 2018) in the statistical software environment *R*. This approach, called indicator saturation, considers a possible outlier or shift at every point in time, but only retains significant indicators. That is how the location-shift lines drawn on Fig. 3.3 were chosen, and is the subject of Chapter 5.

Location shifts are of particular importance in policy, because a policy change inevitably creates a location shift in the system of which it is a part. Consequently, a necessary condition for the policy to have its intended effect is that the parameters in the agency's empirical models of the target variables must remain invariant to that policy shift. Thus, prior to implementing a policy, invariance should be tested, and that can be done automatically as described in Hendry and Santos (2010) and Castle et al. (2017).

4.6 Some Benefits of Non-stationarity

Non-stationarity is pervasive, and as we have documented, needs to be handled carefully to produce viable empirical models, but its occurrence is not all bad news. When time series are I(1), their variance grows over time, which can help establish long-run relationships. Some economists believe that so-called 'observational equivalence'—where several different theories look alike on all data—is an important problem. While that worry could be true in a stationary world, cointegration can only hold between I(1) variables that are genuinely linked. 'Observational equivalence' is also unlikely facing location shifts: no matter how many co-breaking relations exist, there must always be fewer than the number of variables, as some must shift to change others, separating the sheep from the goats.

When I(1) variables also trend, or drift, that can reveal the underlying links between variables even when measurement errors are quite large (see Duffy and Hendry 2017). Those authors also establish the benefits of location shifts that co-break in identifying links between mis-measured variables: intuitively, simultaneous jumps in both variables clarify their connection despite any 'fog' from measurement errors surrounding their relationship. Thus, large shifts can help reveal the linkages between variables, as well as the absence thereof.

Moreover, empirical economics is plagued by very high correlations between variables (as well as over time), but location shifts can substantively reduce such collinearity. In particular, as demonstrated by White and Kennedy (2009), location shifts can play a positive role in clarifying causality. Also, White (2006) uses large location shifts to estimate the effects of natural experiments.

Finally, location shifts also enable powerful tests of the invariance of the parameters of policy models to policy interventions before new policies are implemented, potentially avoiding poor policy outcomes (see Hendry and Santos 2010). Thus, while wide-sense non-stationarity poses problems for economic theories, empirical modelling and forecasting, there are benefits to be gained as well.

Non-stationary time series are the norm in many disciplines including economics, climatology, and demography as illustrated in Figs. 2.3–3.2: the world changes, often in unanticipated ways. Research, and especially policy, must acknowledge the hazards of modelling what we have called wide-sense non-stationary time series, where distributions of outcomes change, as illustrated in Fig. 4.5. Individually and together when stochastic trends and location shifts are not addressed, they can distort in-sample inferences, lead to systematic forecast failure out-of-sample, and substantively increase forecast uncertainty as we will discuss in Chapter 7. However, both forms can be tamed in part using the methods of cointegration and modelling location shifts respectively, as Fig. 4.6 showed.

A key feature of every non-stationary process is that the distribution of outcomes shifts over time, illustrated in Fig. 4.7 for histograms and densities of logs of UK real GDP in each of three 50-year epochs. Consequently, probabilities of events calculated in one time period do not apply in another: recent examples include increasing longevity affecting pension costs, and changes in frequencies of flooding vitiating flood-defence systems.

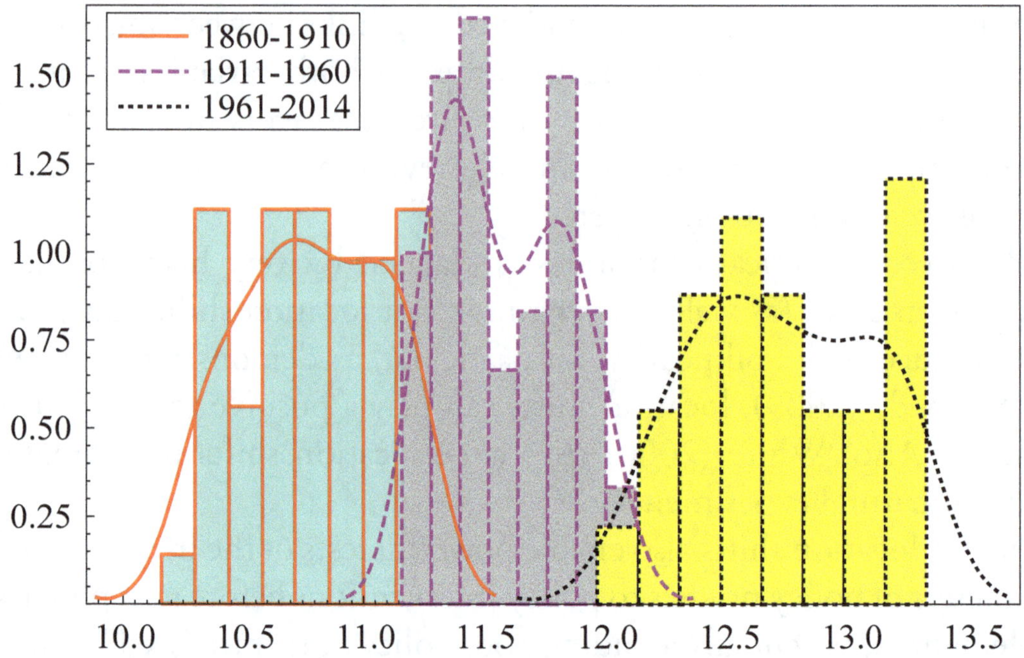

Fig. 4.7 Histograms and densities of logs of UK real GDP in each of three 50-year epochs

The problem of shifts in distributions is not restricted to the levels of variables: distributions of changes can also shift albeit that is more difficult to see in plots like Fig. 4.7. Consequently, Fig. 4.8 shows histograms and densities of changes in UK CO_2 emissions in each of four 40-year epochs in four separate graphs but on common scales for both axes. The shifts are now relatively obvious at least between the top two plots and between pre and post World War II, although the wide horizontal axis makes any shifts between the last two periods less obvious.

Conversely, we noted some benefits of stochastic trends and location shifts as they help reveal genuine links between variables, and also highlight non-constant links, both of which are invaluable knowledge in a policy context.

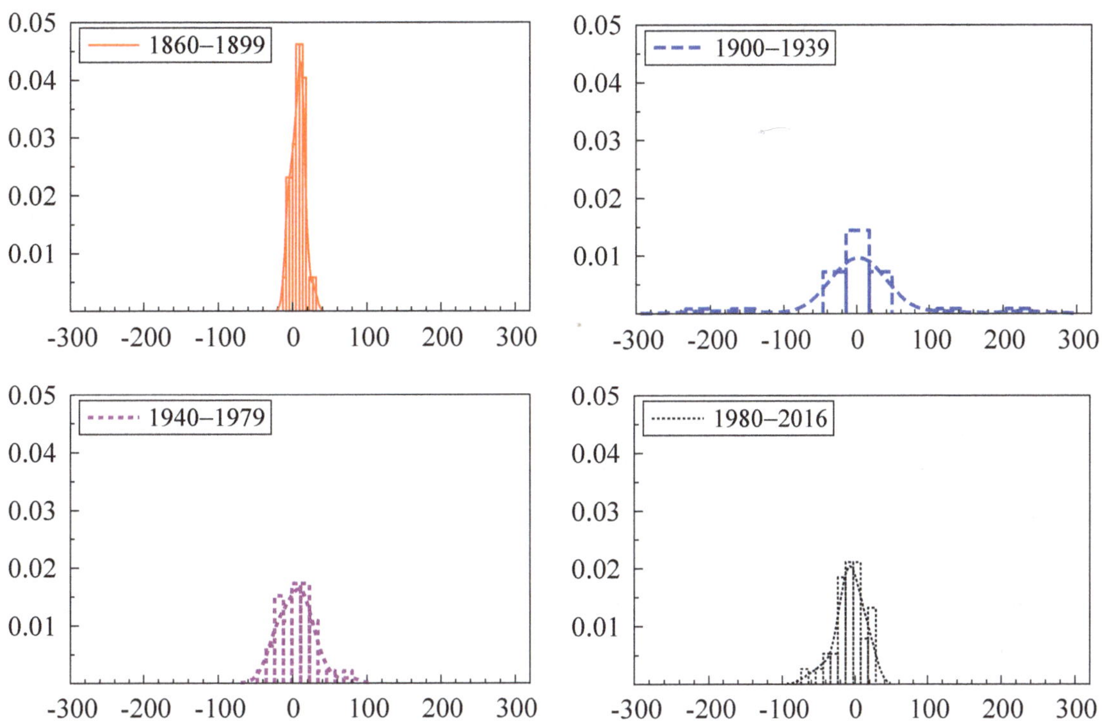

Fig. 4.8 Histograms and densities of changes in UK CO_2 emissions in each of four 40-year epochs

References

Bachelier, L. (1900). Théorie de la spéculation. *Annales Scientifiques de l'École Normale Supérieure*, **3**, 21–86.

Box, G. E. P., and Jenkins, G. M. (1976). *Time Series Analysis, Forecasting and Control.* San Francisco: Holden-Day. First published, 1970.

Castle, J. L., Hendry, D. F., and Martinez, A. B. (2017). Evaluating forecasts, narratives and policy using a test of invariance. *Econometrics*, **5(39)**. https://doi.org/10.3390/econometrics5030039.

Castle, J. L., Doornik, J. A., Hendry, D. F., and Nymoen, R. (2014). Mis-specification testing: Non-invariance of expectations models of inflation. *Econometric Reviews*, **33**, 553–574.

Castle, J. L., Doornik, J. A., Hendry, D. F., and Pretis, F. (2015). Detecting location shifts during model selection by step-indicator saturation. *Econometrics*, **3(2)**, 240–264. http://www.mdpi.com/2225-1146/3/2/240.

Davidson, J. E. H., Hendry, D. F., Srba, F., and Yeo, J. S. (1978). Econometric modelling of the aggregate time-series relationship between consumers' expenditure and income in the United Kingdom. *Economic Journal*, **88**, 661–692.

Doornik, J. A. (2009). Autometrics. In Castle, J. L., and Shephard, N. (eds.), *The Methodology and Practice of Econometrics*, pp. 88–121. Oxford: Oxford University Press.

Duffy, J. A., and Hendry, D. F. (2017). The impact of near-integrated measurement errors on modelling long-run macroeconomic time series. *Econometric Reviews*, **36**, 568–587.

Granger, C. W. J. (1981). Some properties of time series data and their use in econometric model specification. *Journal of Econometrics*, **16**, 121–130.

Hendry, D. F. (1999). An econometric analysis of US food expenditure, 1931–1989. In Magnus, J. R., and Morgan, M. S. (eds.), *Methodology and Tacit Knowledge: Two Experiments in Econometrics*, pp. 341–361. Chichester: Wiley.

Hendry, D. F. (2004). The Nobel Memorial Prize for Clive W.J. Granger. *Scandinavian Journal of Economics*, **106**, 187–213.

Hendry, D. F. (2015). *Introductory Macro-econometrics: A New Approach*. London: Timberlake Consultants. http://www.timberlake.co.uk/macroeconometrics.html.

Hendry, D. F., and Mizon, G. E. (2014). Unpredictability in economic analysis, econometric modeling and forecasting. *Journal of Econometrics*, **182**, 186–195.

Hendry, D. F., and Muellbauer, J. N. J. (2018). The future of macroeconomics: Macro theory and models at the Bank of England. *Oxford Review of Economic Policy*, **34**, 287–328. https://academic.oup.com/oxrep/article/34/1-2/287/4781814.

Hendry, D. F., and Santos, C. (2010). An automatic test of super exogeneity. In Watson, M. W., Bollerslev, T., and Russell, J.(eds.), *Volatility and Time Series Econometrics*, pp. 164–193. Oxford: Oxford University Press.

Johansen, S., and Nielsen, B. (2009). An analysis of the indicator saturation estimator as a robust regression estimator. In Castle, J. L., and Shephard, N. (eds.), *The Methodology and Practice of Econometrics*, pp. 1–36. Oxford: Oxford University Press.

Kaufmann, R. K., Kauppi, H., Mann, M. L., and Stock, J. H. (2013). Does temperature contain a stochastic trend: Linking statistical results to physical mechanisms. *Climatic Change*, **118(3–4)**, 729–743.

Lee, R. D., and Carter, L. R. (1992). Modeling and forecasting U.S. mortality. *Journal of the American Statistical Association*, **87**, 659–671.

Magnus, J. R., and Morgan, M. S. (eds.) (1999). *Methodology and Tacit Knowledge: Two Experiments in Econometrics*. Chichester: Wiley.

Pretis, F. (2019). Econometric models of climate systems: The equivalence of two-component energy balance models and cointegrated VARs. *Journal of Econometrics*. https://doi.org/10.1016/j.jeconom.2019.05.013.

Pretis, F., Reade, J. J., and Sucarrat, G. (2018). Automated general-to-specific (GETS) regression modeling and indicator saturation for outliers and structural breaks. *Journal of Statistical Software*, **68**, 4. https://www.jstatsoft.org/article/view/v086i03.

Soros, G. (2008). *The New Paradigm for Financial Markets.* London: Perseus Books.

Taleb, N. N. (2007). *The Black Swan.* New York: Random House.

White, H. (2006). Time series estimation of the effects of natural experiments. *Journal of Econometrics*, **135**, 527–566.

White, H., and Kennedy, P. (2009). Retrospective estimation of causal effects through time. In Castle, J. L., and Shephard, N. (eds.), *The Methodology and Practice of Econometrics*, pp. 59–87. Oxford: Oxford University Press.

Yule, G. U. (1926). Why do we sometimes get nonsense-correlations between time-series? A study in sampling and the nature of time series (with discussion). *Journal of the Royal Statistical Society*, **89**, 1–64. Reprinted in Hendry, D. F., and Morgan, M. S. (1995). *The Foundations of Econometric Analysis.* Cambridge: Cambridge University Press.

5

Detectives of Change: Indicator Saturation

Abstract Structural changes are pervasive from innovations affecting many disciplines. These can shift distributions, altering relationships and causing forecast failure. Many empirical models also have outliers: both can distort inference. When the dates of shifts are not known, they need to be detected to be handled, usually by creating an indicator variable that matches the event. The basic example is an impulse indicator equal to unity for the date of an outlier and zero elsewhere. We discuss an approach to finding multiple outliers and shifts called saturation estimation. For finding outliers, an impulse indicator is created for every observation and the computer program searches to see which, if any, match an outlier. Similarly for location shifts: a step indicator equal to unity till time t is created for every t and searched over. We explain how and why this approach works.

Keywords Detecting shifts · Indicator saturation methods · Impulse-indicator saturation (IIS) · Step-indicator saturation (SIS) · Outliers · Non-linearity

J. L. Castle and D. F. Hendry, *Modelling our Changing World*,
Palgrave Texts in Econometrics, https://doi.org/10.1007/978-3-030-21432-6_5

Shifting distributions are indicative of structural change, but that can take many forms, from sudden location shifts, changes in trend rates of growth, or in estimated parameters reflecting changes over time in relationships between variables. Further, outliers that could be attributed to specific events, but are not modelled, can lead to seemingly fat-tailed distributions when in fact the underlying process generating the data is thin tailed. Incorrect or changing distributions pose severe problems for modelling any phenomena, and need to be correctly dealt with for viable estimation and inference on parameters of interest. Empirical modelling that does not account for shifts in the distributions of the variables under analysis risks reaching potentially misleading conclusions by wrongly attributing explanations from such contamination to chance correlations with other included variables, as well as having non-constant parameters.

While the dates of some major events like the Great Depression, oil and financial crises, and major wars are known *ex post*, those of many other events are not. Moreover, the durations and magnitudes of the impacts on economies of shifts are almost never known. Consequently, it behoves any investigator of economic (and indeed many other) time series to find and neutralize the impacts of all the in-sample outliers and shifts on the estimates of their parameters of interest. Shifts come at unanticipated times with many different shapes, durations and magnitudes, so general methods to detect them are needed. 'Ocular' approaches to spotting outliers in a model are insufficient: an apparent outlier may be captured by one of the explanatory variables, and the absence of any obvious outliers does not entail that large residuals will not appear after fitting.

It may be thought that the considerable number of tests required to check for outliers and shifts everywhere in a sample might itself be distorting, and hence adversely affect statistical inference. In particular, will one find too many non-existent perturbations by chance? That worry may be exacerbated by the notion of using an indicator saturation approach, where an indicator for a possible outlier or shift at every observation is included in the set of explanatory variables to be searched over. Even if there are just 100 observations, there will be a hundred indicators plus variables, so there are many trillions of combinations of models created by including or omitting each variable and every indicator, be they for outliers or for shifts starting and ending at different times.

Despite the apparent problems, indicator saturation methods can address all of these forms of mis-specification. First developed to detect unknown numbers of outliers of unknown magnitudes at unknown points in the sample, including at the beginning and end of a sample, the method can be generalized to detect all forms of deterministic structural change. We begin by outlining the method of impulse-indicator saturation (IIS) to detect outliers, before demonstrating how the approach can be generalized to include step, trend, multiplicative and designer saturation. We then briefly discuss how to distinguish between non-linearity and structural change.

Saturation methods can detect multiple breaks, and have the additional benefit that they can be undertaken conjointly with all other aspects of model selection. Explanatory variables, dynamics and non-linearities can be selected jointly with indicators for unknown breaks and outliers. Such a 'portmanteau' approach to detecting breaks while also selecting over many candidate variables is essential when the underlying DGP is unknown and has to be discovered from the available evidence. Most other break detection methods rely on assuming the model is somehow correctly specified other than the breaks, and such methods can lack power to detect breaks if the model is far from 'correct', an event that will occur with high probability in non-stationary time series.

5.1 Impulse-Indicator Saturation

IIS creates a complete set of indicator variables. Each indicator takes the value 1 for a single observation, and 0 for all other observations. As many indicators as there are observations are created, each with a different observation corresponding to the value 1. So for a sample of T observations, T indicators are then included in the set of candidate variables. However, all those indicators are most certainly **not** included together in the regression, as otherwise a perfect fit would always result and nothing would be learned. Although saturation creates T additional variables when there are T observations, *Autometrics* provides an expanding and contracting block search algorithm to undertake model selection when there are more variables than observations, as discussed in the model selection primer in Chapter 2. To aid exposition, we shall outline the 'split-half' approach analyzed in Hendry et al. (2008), which is just the simplest way to explain and analyze IIS, so bear in mind that such an approach can be generalized to a larger number of possibly unequal 'splits', and that the software explores many paths.

Defining Indicators
Impulse indicators are defined as $\{1_{\{j=t\}}\}$ where $1_{\{j=t\}}$ is equal to unity when $j = t$ and equal to zero otherwise for $j = 1, \ldots, T$.

Including an impulse indicator for a particular observation in a static regression delivers the same estimate of the model's parameters as if that observation had been left out. Consequently, the coefficient of that indicator is equal to the residual of the associated observation when predicted from a model based on the other observations. In dynamic relations, omitting an observation can distort autocorrelations, but an impulse indicator will simply deliver a zero residual at that observation. Thus, in both cases, including $T/2$ indicators provides estimates of the model based on the other half of the observations. Moreover, we get an estimate of any discrepancies in that half of the observations relative to the other half. Those indicators can then be tested for significance using the estimated error variance from the other half as the baseline, and any significant indicators are recorded. Importantly, under the null, each half's estimates of parameters and error variance are unbiased.

To understand the 'split-half' approach, consider a linear regression that only includes an intercept, to which we add the first $T/2$ impulse indicators, although there are in fact no outliers. Doing so has the same effect as dummying out the first half of the observations such that unbiased estimates of the mean and variance are obtained from the remaining data. Any observations in the first half that are discrepant relative to those estimates at the chosen significance level, α, say 1%, will result in selected indicators. The locations of any significant indicators are recorded, then the first $T/2$ indicators are replaced by the second $T/2$, and the procedure repeated. The two sets of sub-sample significant indicators (if any) are added to the model for selection of the finally significant indicators. This step is not superfluous: when there is a location shift, for example, some

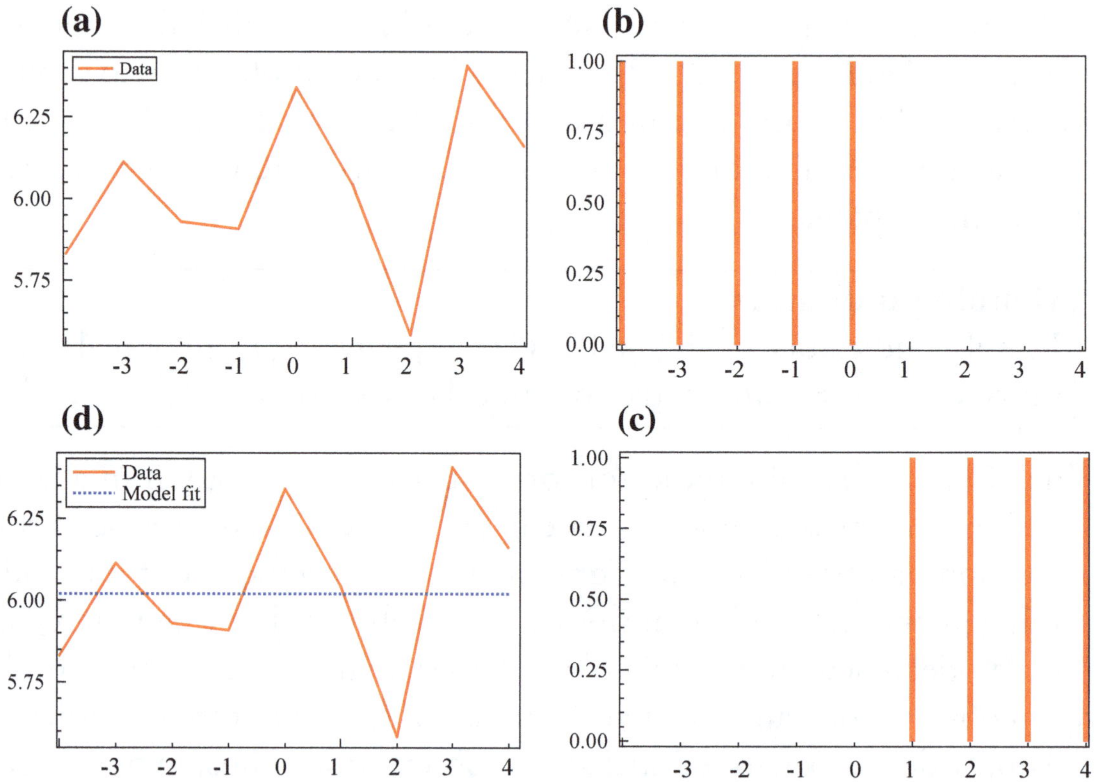

Fig. 5.1 'Split-half' IIS search under null. (**a**) The data time series; (**b**) the first 5 impulse indicators included; (**c**) the other set of impulse indicators; (**d**) the outcome, as no indicators are selected

indicators may be significant as approximations to the shift, but become insignificant when the correct indicators are included.

Figure 5.1 illustrates the 'split-half' approach when $T = 9$ for an independent, identically distributed (IID) Normal random variable with a mean of 6.0 and a variance of 0.33. Impulse indicators will be selected at the significance level $\alpha = 0.05$.

> **Computer Generated Data**
> The IID Normal variable is denoted by $y_t \sim \mathsf{IN}[\mu, \sigma_y^2]$, where μ is the mean and σ_y^2 is the variance. A random number generator on a computer creates an $\mathsf{IN}[0, 1]$ series which is then scaled appropriately.

Figure 5.1(a) shows the data time series, where the dating relates to periods before and after a shift described below. Then panels (b) and (c) record which of the 9 impulse indicators were included in turn, then panel

(d) shows the outcome, where the fitted model is just a constant as no indicators are selected. Since $\alpha T = 0.05 \times 9 = 0.45$, that is the average null retention rate, where α is called the theoretical gauge, which measures a key property of the procedure. This implies that we expect about one irrelevant indicator to be retained every *second* time IIS is applied to $T = 9$ observations using $\alpha = 0.05$ when the null is true, so finding none is not a surprise.

Hendry et al. (2008) establish a feasible algorithm for IIS, and derive its null distribution for an **IID** process. Johansen and Nielsen (2009) extend those findings to general dynamic regression models (possibly with trends or unit roots), and show that the distributions of regression parameter estimates remain almost unaltered, despite investigating the potential relevance of T additional indicators, with a small efficiency loss under the null of no breaks when αT is small. For a stationary process, with a correct null of no outliers and a symmetric error distribution, under relatively weak assumptions, the limiting distribution of the estimators of the regression parameters of interest converges to the population parameters at the usual rate (namely $\sqrt{T}$) despite using IIS. Moreover, that is still a Normal distribution, where the variance is somewhat larger than the conventional form, determined by the stringency of the significance level used for retaining impulse indicators. For example, using a 1% significance level, the estimator variance will be around 1% larger.

If the significance level is set to the inverse of the sample size, $1/T$, only one irrelevant indicator will be retained on average by chance, entailing that just one observation will be 'dummied out'. Think of it: IIS allows us to examine T impulse indicators for their significance almost costlessly when they are not needed. Yet IIS has also checked for the possibility of an unknown number of outliers, of unknown magnitudes and unknown signs, not knowing in advance where in the data set they occurred!

The empirical gauge g is the fraction of incorrectly retained variables, so here is the number of indicators retained under the null divided by T. More generally, if on average one irrelevant variable in a hundred is adventitiously retained in the final selection, the empirical gauge is $g = 0.01$. Johansen and Nielsen (2016) derive its distribution, and show g is close to α for small α. IIS has a close affinity to robust statistics, which is not surprising as it seeks to prevent outliers from contaminating estimates of parameters of interest. Thus, they also demonstrate that IIS is a member of the class of robust estimators, being a special case of a 1-step Huber-skip estimator when the model specification is known.

Illustrating IIS for an Outlier
We generate an outlier of size λ at observation k by $y_t = \mu + \lambda 1_{\{t=k\}} + \varepsilon_t$ where $\varepsilon_t \sim \mathsf{IN}\left[0, \sigma_\varepsilon^2\right]$ and $\lambda \neq 0$.

To illustrate 'split-half' IIS search under the alternative (i.e., when there is an outlier as in the box), Fig. 5.2 records the behaviour of IIS for an outlier of $\lambda = -1.0$ at observation $k = 1$, so earlier dates are shown as negative. Selecting at $\alpha = 0.05$, no first-half indicators are retained (Fig. 5.2 panel (b)), as the discrepancy between the first-half and second-half means is not large relative to the resulting variance. When those indicators are

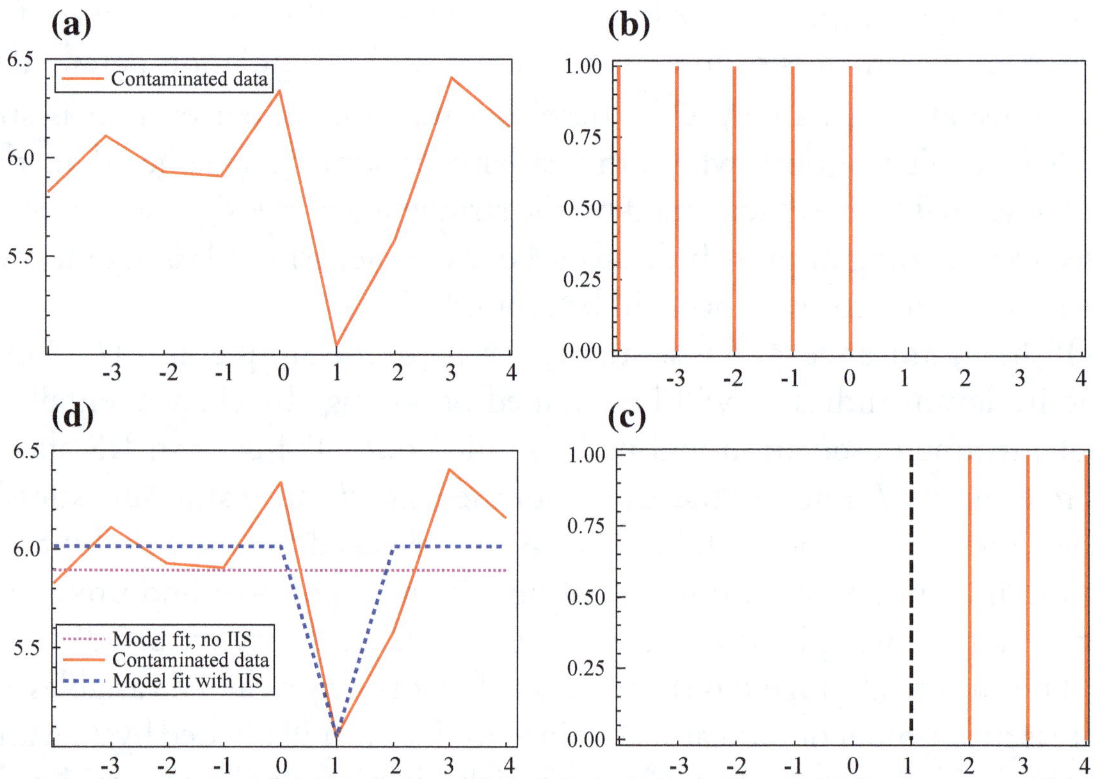

Fig. 5.2 (a) Perturbed data time series; (b) the first 5 impulse indicators included; (c) the other set of impulse indicators where the dashed line indicates retained; (d) the outcome with and without the selected indicator

dropped and the second set entered, the first for the period after the outlier is now retained: note that the first-half variance is very small.

Here the combined set is also just the second selection. When the null of no outliers or breaks is true, any indicator that is significant on a sub-sample would remain so overall, but for many alternatives, sub-sample significance can be transient, due to an unmodelled feature that occurs elsewhere in the data set.

Despite its apparently arcane formulation involving more variables plus indicators than available observations, the properties of which we discussed above, IIS is closely related to a number of other well-known statistical approaches. First, consider recursive estimation, where a model is fitted to a small initial subset of the data, say $K > N$ values when there are N variables, then observations are added one at a time to check for changes in parameter estimates. In IIS terms, this is equivalent to starting with impulse indicators for the last $T - K$ observations, then dropping those indicators one at a time as each next observation is included in the recursion.

Second, rolling regressions, where a fixed sample length is used, so earlier observations are dropped as later ones are added, is a further special case, equivalent to sequentially adding impulse indicators to eliminate earlier observations and dropping those for later.

Third, investigators sometimes drop observations or truncate their sample for what they view as discrepant periods such as wars. Again, this is a special case of IIS, namely including impulse indicators for the observations to be eliminated, precisely as we discussed above for modelling US food demand from 1929 to 1952. A key lack in all these methods is not inspecting the indicators for their significance or information content. However, because the variation in such apparently 'discrepant' periods can be invaluable in breaking collinearities and enhancing estimation precision, much can be learned by applying IIS instead, and checking which, if any, observations are actually problematic, perhaps using archival research to find out why.

Fourth, the Chow test for parameter constancy can be implemented by adding impulse indicators for the subsample to be tested, clearly a special case of IIS. Thus, IIS nests all of these settings. There is a large literature on testing for a known number of breaks, but indicator saturation is applicable when there is an unknown number of outliers or shifts, and can be implemented jointly with selecting over other regressors. Instrumental variables variants follow naturally, with the added possibility of checking the instrument equations for outliers and shifts, leading to being able to test the specification of the equation of interest for invariance to shifts in the instruments.

IIS is **designed** to detect outliers rather than location shifts, but split-half can also be used to illustrate indicator saturation when there is a single location shift which lies entirely within one of the halves. For a single location shift, Hendry and Santos (2010) show that the detection power, or potency, of IIS is determined by the magnitude of the shift; the length of the break interval, which determines how many indicators need to be found; the error variance of the equation; and the significance level, α, as a Normal-distribution critical value, c_α, is used by the IIS selection algorithm. Castle et al. (2012) establish the ability of IIS in *Autometrics* to detect multiple location shifts and outliers, including breaks close to the start and end of the sample, as well as correcting for non-Normality. Nevertheless, we next consider step-indicator saturation, which is explicitly designed for detecting location shifts.

5.2 Step-Indicator Saturation

A step shift is just a block of contiguous impulses of the same signs and magnitudes. Although IIS is applicable to detecting these, then the retained indicators could be combined into one dummy variable taking the average value of the shift over the break period and 0 elsewhere, perhaps after conducting a joint F-test on the *ex post* equality of the retained IIS coefficients, there is a more efficient method for detecting step shifts. We can instead generate a saturating set of $T - 1$ step-shift indicators which take the value 1 from the beginning of the sample up to a given observation, and 0 thereafter, with each step switching from 1 to 0 at a different observation. Step indicators are the cumulation of impulse indicators up to each next observation. The 'T'th step would just be the intercept. The $T - 1$ steps are included in the set of candidate regressors.

The split-half algorithm is conducted in exactly the same way, but there are some differences.

> **Defining Step Indicators**
> Step indicators are defined by $1_{\{t \leq j\}}$, $j = 1, \ldots, T$, where $1_{\{t \leq j\}} = 1$ for observations up to j, and zero otherwise.

First, while impulse indicators are mutually orthogonal, step indicators overlap increasingly as their second index increases. Second, for a location shift that is not at either end, say from T_1 to T_2, two indicators are required to characterize it: $1_{\{t \leq T_2\}} - 1_{\{t < T_1\}}$. Third, for a split-half analysis, the ease of detection is affected by whether or not T_1 and T_2 lie in the same split, and whether location shifts occur in both halves with similar signs and magnitudes. Castle et al. (2015) derive the null retention frequency of SIS and demonstrate the improved potency relative to IIS for longer location shifts.

We now consider 'split-sample' SIS for the same data as used for IIS above. As it happens, the second half coincides with the break period, so rather than use the first and second halves, we illustrate 'half-sample' SIS, where some indicators are chosen from each half as shown in Fig. 5.3 under the null. As *Autometrics* software uses multi-path block searches, this choice is potentially one of many paths explored, so has no specific advantage, but hopefully avoids the impression that the method is successful because the shift neatly coincides with the second half.

Figure 5.3 panel (a) records the time series; panels (b) and (c) the first and second choices of the 9 step indicators where now solid, dotted, dashed and long dashed clarify the steps, and panel (d) reports the same outcome as for IIS, as no indicators are selected.

> **Illustrating SIS for a Location Shift**
> Here we generate a location shift of magnitude λ at observation k by $y_t = \mu + \lambda 1_{\{t \geq k\}} + \varepsilon_t$ where $\varepsilon_t \sim \mathsf{IN}\left[0, \sigma_\varepsilon^2\right]$ and $\lambda \neq 0$.

Next, we modify the process that generated an outlier to instead generate a location shift of $\lambda = -1$ at $k = 0$, but with the same half selections of step indicators. Figure 5.4 illustrates the outcome. Panel (a) records the shifted data, (b) shows the first selection of step indicators and (c) the remainder

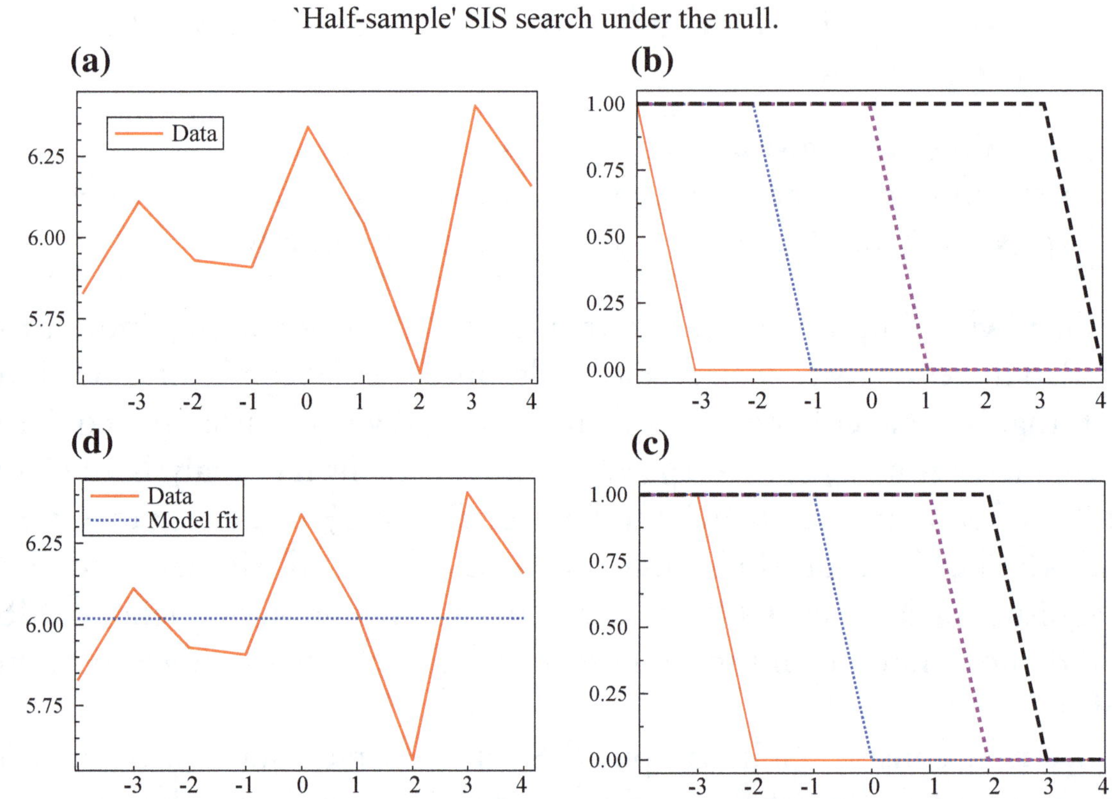

Fig. 5.3 **(a)** The data time series; **(b)** the 4 step indicators included; **(c)** the other set of step indicators; **(d)** the outcome as no indicators are selected

where now the thick solid line denotes the selected indicator, with (d) showing the outcome with and without that selected step indicator.

Notice how the fit without handling the shift produces 'spurious' residual autocorrelation, as all the residuals are first positive, then all become negative after observation 1. 'Treating' the residual autocorrelation by a conventional recipe would not be a good solution (see Mizon 1995) as the location shift is not correctly modelled. Finally, a more parsimonious and less 'overfitted' outcome results than would be found using IIS which would produce a perfect fit to the last 4 data points.

Figure 4.6 for the growth of real wages was used to illustrate co-breaking between wage growth and inflation, both of which experienced myriad shifts. However, the graph hides that the latter half of the twentieth century had a substantively higher mean real-wage growth at 1.8% p.a. post-1945 versus 0.7% p.a. pre, and 1.3% overall. Real wages would have increased 16-fold at 1.8% p.a. from 1860, rather than just threefold at 0.7% p.a.,

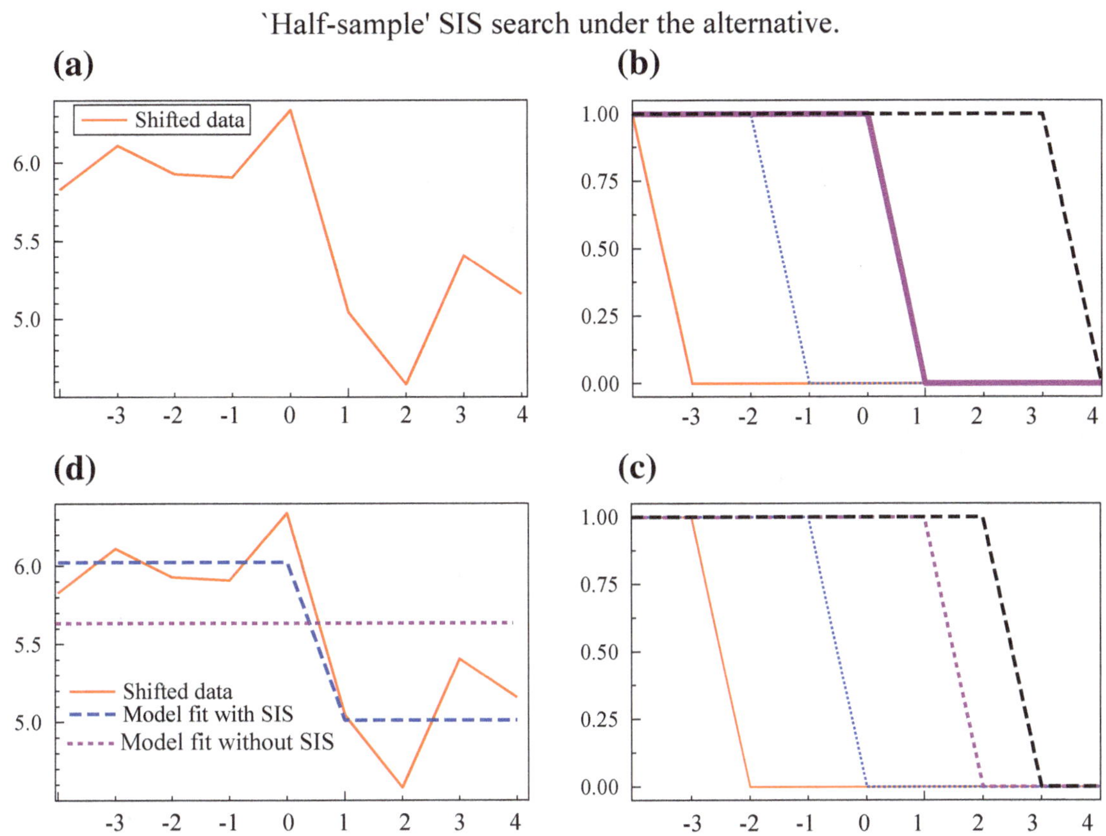

Fig. 5.4 (**a**) The shifted time series; (**b**) the first 4 step indicators included where the thick solid line denotes selected; (**c**) the other 4 step indicators; (**d**) the outcome with the selected step indicator

and sevenfold in practice: 'small' changes in growth rates can dramatically alter living standards. The location shifts shown on the graph were selected by SIS at $\alpha = 0.005$, and were not noticed, or included, in earlier models, but helped clarify the many influences on real wages (see Castle and Hendry 2014).

5.3 Designing Indicator Saturation

But why stop at step-indicator saturation? A location shift in the growth rate of a variable must imply that there is a change in the trend of the variable itself.

5.3.1 Trend-Indicator Saturation

Thus, one way of capturing a trend break would be to saturate the model with a series of trend indicators, which generate a trend up to a given observation and 0 thereafter for every observation. However, trend breaks can be difficult to detect as small changes in trends can take time to accumulate, even if they eventually lead to very substantial differences.

> **Defining Trend Indicators**
> Trend indicators are defined as $\mathsf{T}_{jt} = t - j + 1$ for $t \geq j,\ j = 1, \ldots, T$ and 0 otherwise.

Figure 5.5 also illustrated the issue that although the long-run effect of the step shift detected by SIS starting in 1945 was dramatic, that would not have been clear at the time. The average growth of 1.4% p.a. over the first 15 years, 1945–1960, after SIS detects the shift, is little different from the 1.2% p.a. near the start of data period over the 15 years 1864–1879. Indeed, fitting SIS to the sample up to 1960, it finds a location shift from 1944 of 1.1% which could be the end of a World War II effect rather than the start of the prolonged higher growth to come.

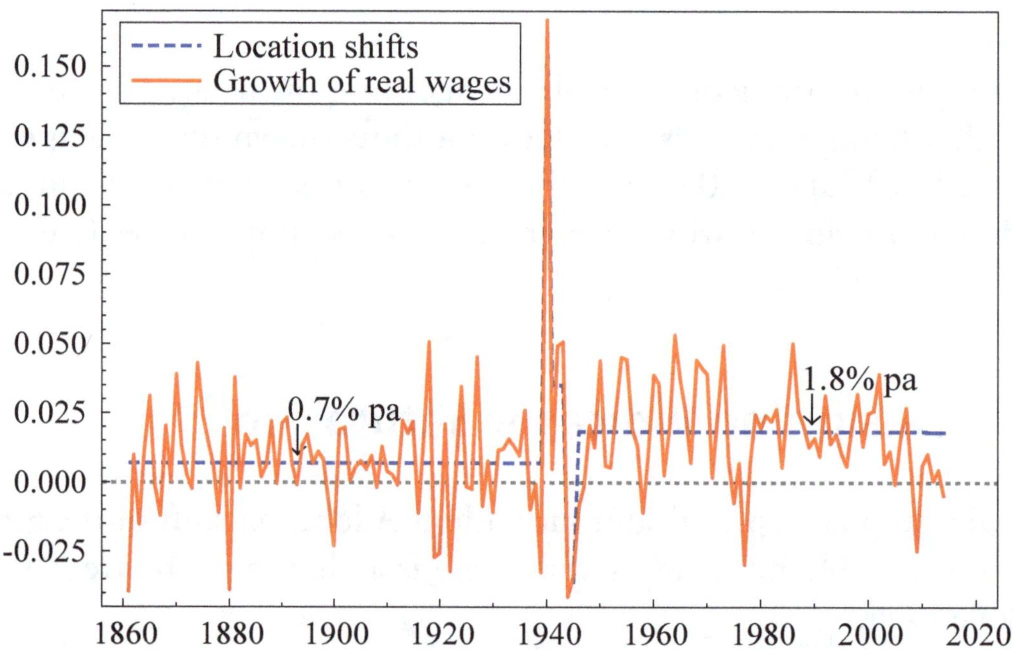

Fig. 5.5 A location shift in the growth of UK real wages

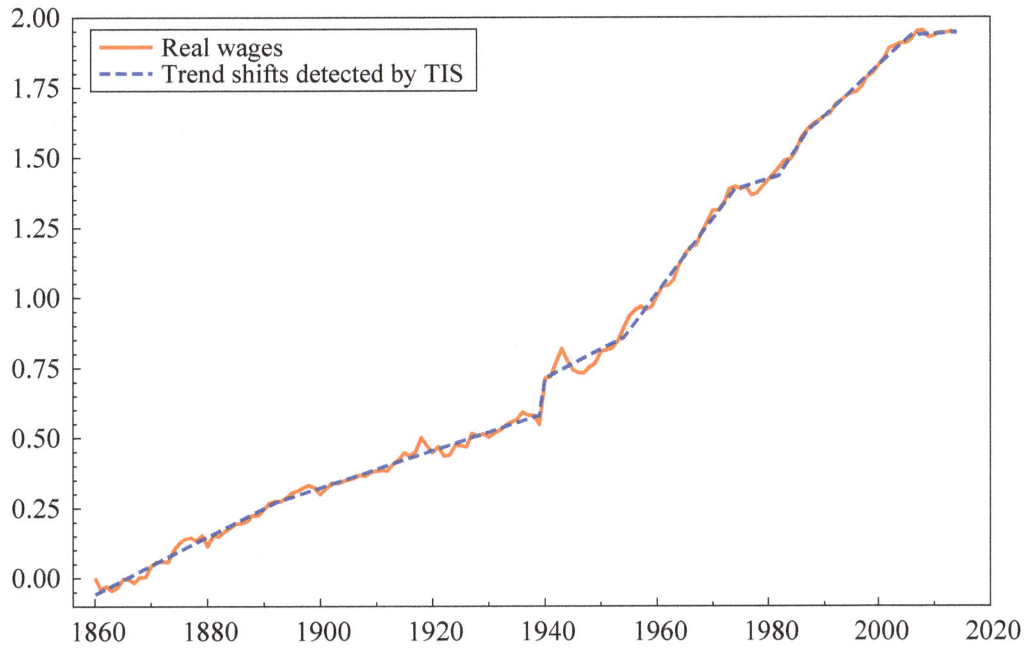

Fig. 5.6 Several trend breaks in UK real wages detected by TIS

We illustrate trend-indicator saturation (TIS) for the level of real wages as shown in Fig. 5.6. Selection was undertaken at $\alpha = 0.001$, using such a tight significance level because the variable is I(1) with shifts, so considerable residual serial correlation seemed likely. An overall trend was retained without selection, so deviations therefrom were being detected. Even at such a tight significance level, nine trend indicators were retained, several acting for short periods, as with the jump between 1939 and 1940 (matching the spike in Fig. 5.5), and the flattening over 1973–1981, and again at the end of the period.

5.3.2 Multiplicative-Indicator Saturation

Ericsson (2012) considered a wide range of possible indicator saturation methods, including combining IIS and SIS (super saturation) and multiplicative-indicator saturation (MIS) where every variable in a candidate set is multiplied by every step indicator. For example, with 100 observations and four regressor variables there will be 400 candidates to select from. Kitov and Tabor (2015) have investigated the properties of

MIS by simulation, and found it can detect shifts in regression parameters despite the huge number of candidate variables. This prompted Castle et al. (2017) to apply the approach to successfully detect induced shifts in estimated models following a policy intervention. They offer an explanation for the surprisingly good performance of MIS as follows. Imagine knowing where a shift occurred, so you split your data sample at that point and fit the now correctly specified model separately to the two sub-samples. You would be deservedly surprised if those appropriate sub-sample estimates did not reflect the parameter shifts. Choosing the split by MIS will add variability, but the correct indicator, or one close to it, should be selected as that is where the parameters changed. Of course, as ever with model selection, 'unlucky' draws from the error distribution may make the shift appear to happen slightly earlier or later than actually occurred. We consider an application of MIS in the next Chapter.

5.3.3 Designed-Break Indicator Saturation

If the breaks under investigation have a relatively regular shape, saturation techniques can be 'designed' appropriately, denoted DIS. This idea has been used by Pretis et al. (2016) to detect the impacts of volcanic eruptions on temperature records. When a volcano erupts, it spews material into the atmosphere and above, which can 'block' sunlight, or more accurately, reduce received solar radiation. The larger the eruption, the more solar radiation is reduced. Thus, the eruption of Tambora in 1816 created the 'year without a summer' in the Northern Hemisphere, adding to the difficulties people confronted just after the end of the Napoleonic wars. More generally, atmospheric temperatures drop rapidly during and immediately after an eruption, then as the ejected material is removed from the atmosphere, temperature slowly recovers, like a 'ν'. Thus, a saturating set of indicators with such a shape can be created and applied to the relevant time series, selecting rather like we described above for SIS. The follow up in Schneider et al. (2017) demonstrates the success of DIS for detecting the impacts of volcanic eruptions to improve dendrochronological temperature reconstructions.

5.4 Outliers and Non-linearity

The methods discussed above were designed to detect unknown outliers (IIS), location shifts (SIS), trend breaks (TIS), parameter changes (MIS) and volcanic eruptions (DIS) that actually happened, at a pre-set significance level. An alternative explanation for what appears to be structural change is that the data generating process is non-linear. Possible examples include Markov switching models (see e.g., Hamilton 1989), threshold (see e.g., Priestley 1981) and smooth transition models (see e.g., Granger Teräsvirta 1993), where the non-linearity is 'regular' in some way. Distinguishing between the two explanations can be difficult. Indeed, non-linearities and deterministic structural breaks can often be closely similar. But a key advantage of *Autometrics* is that it operates as a variable selection algorithm, allowing selection over non-linear functions as well as potential outliers and breaks, so both explanations can be tested jointly, and both explanations could well play a role in explaining the phenomena of interest.

The *Autometrics*-based approach in Castle and Hendry (2014) creates a class of non-linear functions from transformations of the original data variables to approximate a wide range of potential non-linearities in a low-dimensional way. The problem with including, say, a general cubic function of all the (non-indicator) candidate variables is the explosion in the number of terms that need to be considered. For example, with 20 candidates, there are 1539 cubic terms. However, their simplification adds only 60 terms, at the possible risk of not capturing all the non-linearity in some settings. When an investigator has a specific non-linear function as a preferred explanation, that can be tested against the selected model by encompassing to see if (a) the proposed function is significant, and if so (b) whether it eliminates all the other non-linear terms.

References

Castle, J. L., Doornik, J. A., and Hendry, D. F. (2012). Model selection when there are multiple breaks. *Journal of Econometrics*, **169**, 239–246.

Castle, J. L., Doornik, J. A., Hendry, D. F., and Pretis, F. (2015). Detecting location shifts during model selection by step-indicator saturation. *Econometrics*, **3(2)**, 240–264. http://www.mdpi.com/2225-1146/3/2/240.

Castle, J. L., and Hendry, D. F. (2014). Semi-automatic non-linear model selection. In Haldrup, N., Meitz, M., and Saikkonen, P. (eds.), *Essays in Nonlinear Time Series Econometrics*, pp. 163–197. Oxford: Oxford University Press.

Castle, J. L., Hendry, D. F., and Martinez, A. B. (2017). Evaluating forecasts, narratives and policy using a test of invariance. *Econometrics*, **5(39)**. https://doi.org/10.3390/econometrics5030039.

Ericsson, N. R. (2012). Detecting crises, jumps, and changes in regime. Working paper, Federal Reserve Board of Governors, Washington, DC.

Granger, C. W. J., and Teräsvirta, T. (1993). *Modelling Nonlinear Economic Relationships*. Oxford: Oxford University Press.

Hamilton, J. D. (1989). A new approach to economic analysis of nonstationary time series. *Econometrica*, **57**, 357–384.

Hendry, D. F., Johansen, S., and Santos, C. (2008). Automatic selection of indicators in a fully saturated regression. *Computational Statistics*, **33**, 317–335. Erratum, 337–339.

Hendry, D. F., and Santos, C. (2010). An automatic test of super exogeneity. In Watson, M. W., Bollerslev, T., and Russell, J. (eds.), *Volatility and Time Series Econometrics*, pp. 164–193. Oxford: Oxford University Press.

Johansen, S., and Nielsen, B. (2009). An analysis of the indicator saturation estimator as a robust regression estimator. In Castle, J. L., and Shephard, N. (eds.), *The Methodology and Practice of Econometrics*, pp. 1–36. Oxford: Oxford University Press.

Johansen, S., and Nielsen, B. (2016). Asymptotic theory of outlier detection algorithms for linear time series regression models. *Scandinavian Journal of Statistics*, **43**, 321–348.

Kitov, O. I., and Tabor, M. N. (2015). Detecting structural changes in linear models: A variable selection approach using multiplicative indicator saturation. Unpublished paper, University of Oxford.

Mizon, G. E. (1995). A simple message for autocorrelation correctors: Don't. *Journal of Econometrics*, **69**, 267–288.

Pretis, F., Schneider, L., Smerdon, J. E., and Hendry, D. F. (2016). Detecting volcanic eruptions in temperature reconstructions by designed break-indicator saturation. *Journal of Economic Surveys*, **30**, 403–429.

Priestley, M. B. (1981). *Spectral Analysis and Time Series*. New York: Academic Press.

Schneider, L., Smerdon, J. E., Pretis, F., Hartl-Meier, C., and Esper, J. (2017). A new archive of large volcanic events over the past millennium derived from reconstructed summer temperatures. *Environmental Research Letters*, **12(9)**. https://doi.org/10.1088/1748-9326/aa7a1b/meta.

6

The Polymath: Combining Theory and Data

Abstract There are numerous possible approaches to building a model of a given data set, whether it be time series, cross section or panel. In economics, imposing a 'theory model' on the data, by simply estimating its parameters, is common. In 'big data' analyses, various methods of selecting relationships are used (aka 'data mining'), but in practice, modellers often select equations from data using theory-based guidelines. We discuss an approach that can retain all available theory information unaffected by selecting over additional candidate variables, lags (for time series), and non-linear functions, taking account of both potential outliers and shifts, yet can deliver an improved model when the theory specification is incomplete, incorrect, or changes over time.

Keywords Theory driven · Data driven · Evaluation · Discovery · Modelling inflation

J. L. Castle and D. F. Hendry, *Modelling our Changing World*,
Palgrave Texts in Econometrics, https://doi.org/10.1007/978-3-030-21432-6_6

6.1 Theory Driven and Data Driven Models

Two main approaches to empirically modelling a relationship are purely theory driven and purely data driven. In the former, common in economics, the putative relation is derived from a theoretical analysis claimed to represent the relevant situation, then its parameters are estimated by imposing that 'theory model' on the data.

> **Theory Driven Modelling**
> Let y_t denote the variable to be modelled by a set of n explanatory variables $\mathbf{z}_t$ when the theory relation is $y_t = f(\mathbf{z}_t)$,
> then the parameters of the known function $f(\cdot)$ are estimated from a sample of data over $t = 1, \ldots, T$.

In what follows, we will use a simple aggregate example based on the theory-model that monetary expansion causes inflation, reflecting Friedman's claim: 'inflation is always and everywhere a monetary phenomenon'. While it is certainly true that sufficiently large money growth can cause inflation (as in the Hungarian hyperinflation of 1945–1946), it need not do so, as the vast increase in the US monetary base from Quantitative Easing has shown, with the Federal Reserve System balances expanding by several \$trillion. Thus, our dependent variable (y_t) is the rate of inflation, related by a linear function ($f(\cdot)$), in the simplest setting to the growth rate of the money stock together with lagged values of inflation and money growth ($\mathbf{z}_t$) to reflect non-instantaneous adjustments. Previous research has established that 'narrow money' (technically called M1 for currency in circulation plus chequing accounts) does not cause inflation in the UK, so instead we consider the growth in 'broad money' (technically M4, comprising all bank deposits, although the long-run series used here is spliced *ex post* from M2, M3 and M4 as the financial system and measurements evolved over time).

In a data-driven approach, observations on a larger set of $N > n$ variables (denoted $\{\mathbf{x}_t\}$) are collected to 'explain' y_t, which here could augment money with interest rates, growth in GDP and the National Debt, excess demand for goods and services, inflation in wages and other costs, changes in the exchange rate, changes in the unemployment rate, imported inflation, etc. To avoid simultaneous relations, where a variable is affected by inflation, all of these additional possible explanations will be entered lagged. The choice of additional candidate variables is based on looser theoretical guidelines, then some method of model selection is applied to pick the 'best' relation between y_t and a subset of the $\{\mathbf{x}_t\}$ within a class of functional connections (such as a linear relation with constant parameters and small, identically-distributed errors e_t independent of the $\{\mathbf{x}_t\}$). When N is very large ('big data', which could include micro-level data on household characteristics or internet search data), most current approaches have difficulties either in controlling the number of spurious relationships that might be found (because of an actual or implicit significance level for hypothesis tests that is too loose for the magnitude of N), or in retaining all of the relevant explanatory variables with a high probability (because the significance level is too stringent): see e.g., Doornik and Hendry (2015). Moreover, the selected model may be hard to interpret, and if many equations have been tried (but perhaps not reported), the statistical properties of the resulting selected model are unclear: see Leamer (1983).

6.2 The Drawbacks of Using Each Approach in Isolation

Many variants of theory-driven and data-driven approaches exist, often combined with testing the properties of the e_t, the assumptions about the regressors, and the constancy of the relationship $f(\cdot)$, but with different strategies for how to proceed if any of the conditions required for viable inference are rejected. The assumption made all too often is that a rejection occurs because that test has power under the specific alternative for which the test is derived, although a given test can reject for many other reasons. The classic example of such a 'recipe' is finding residual autocorrelation and assuming it arose from error autocorrelation, whereas the problem could be mis-specified dynamics, unmodelled location shifts as seen above, or omitted autocorrelated variables. In our inflation example, in order to eliminate autocorrelation, annual dynamics need to be modelled, along with shifts due to wars, crises and legislative changes. The approach proposed in the next section instead seeks to include all likely determinants from the outset, and would revise the initial general formulation if any of the mis-specification tests thereof rejected.

Most observational data are affected by many influences, often outside the relevant subject's purview—as the 2016 Brexit vote has emphasized for economics—and it would require a brilliant theoretical analysis to take all the substantively important forces into account. Thus, a purely theory-driven approach, such as a monetary theory of aggregate inflation, is unlikely to deliver a complete, correct and immutable model that forges a new 'law' once estimated. Rather, to capture the complexities of real world data, features outside the theory remit almost always need to be taken into account, especially changes resulting from unpredicted events. Moreover, few theories include all the variables that characterize a process, with correct dynamic reactions, and the actual non-linear connections. In addition, the data may be mis-measured for the theory variables (revealed by revising national accounts data as new information accrues), and may even be incorrectly recorded relative to its own definition, leading to outliers. Finally, shifts in relationships are all too common—there is a distinct lack of empirical models that have stood the test of time or have an unblemished forecasting track record: see Hendry and Pretis (2016).

Many of the same problems affect a purely data-driven approach unless the $\mathbf{x}_t$ provide a remarkably comprehensive specification, in which case there will often be more candidate variables N than observations T: see Castle and Hendry (2014) for a discussion of that setting. Because included regressors will 'pick up' influences from any correlated missing variables, omitting important factors usually entails biased parameter estimates, badly behaved residuals, and most importantly, often non-constant models. Failing to retain relevant theory-based variables can be pernicious and potentially distort which models are selected. Thus, an approach that retains, but does not impose, theory-driven variables without affecting the estimates of a correct, complete, and constant theory model, has much to offer, if it also allows selection over a much larger set of candidate variables, avoiding the substantial costs when relevant variables are omitted from the initial specification. We now describe how the benefits of the two approaches can be combined to achieve that outcome based on Hendry and Doornik (2014) and Hendry and Johansen (2015).

6.3 A Combined Approach

Let us assume that the theory correctly specifies the set of relevant variables. This could include lags of the variables to represent an equilibrium-correction mechanism. In the combined approach, the theory relation is retained while selecting over an additional set of potentially relevant candidate variables. These additional candidate variables could include disaggregates for household characteristics (in panel data), as well as the variables noted above. To ensure an encompassing explanation, the additional set of variables could also include additional lags and non-linear functions of the theory variables, other explanatory variables used by different investigators, and indicator variables to capture outliers and shifts.

The general unrestricted model (GUM) is formulated to nest both the theory model and the data-driven formulation. As the theory variables and additional variables are likely to be quite highly correlated, even if the theory model is exactly correct the model estimates are unlikely to be the same as those from estimating the theory model directly. However, the theory variables can be orthogonalized with respect to the additional variables, which means that they are uncorrelated with the other variables. Therefore, inclusion of additional regressors will not affect the estimates of the theory variables in the model, regardless of whether any, or all, of the additional variables are included. The theory variables are always included in the model, and any additional variables can be selected over to see if they are useful in explaining the phenomona of interest. Thus, data-based model selection can be applied to all the potentially relevant candidate explanatory variables while retaining the theory model without selection.

Summary of the Combined Approach
The theory variables are given by the set $\mathbf{z}_t$ of n relevant variables entering $f(\cdot)$. We use the explicit parametrization for $f(\cdot)$ of a linear, constant parameter vector $\boldsymbol{\beta}$, so the theory model is:
$y_t = \boldsymbol{\beta}'\mathbf{z}_t + e_t$,
where $e_t \sim \mathsf{IN}[0, \sigma_e^2]$ is independent of $\mathbf{z}_t$.
Define the additional set of M candidate variables as $\{\mathbf{w}_t\}$.

Formulate the GUM as:
$y_t = \boldsymbol{\beta}'\mathbf{z}_t + \boldsymbol{\gamma}'\mathbf{w}_t + v_t$,
which nests both the theory model and the data-driven formulation when $\mathbf{x}_t = (\mathbf{z}_t, \mathbf{w}_t)$, so v_t will inherit the properties of e_t when $\boldsymbol{\gamma} = \mathbf{0}$.

Without loss of generality, $\mathbf{z}_t$ can be orthogonalized with respect to $\mathbf{w}_t$ by projecting the latter onto the former in:
$\mathbf{w}_t = \boldsymbol{\Gamma}\mathbf{z}_t + \mathbf{u}_t$
where $\mathsf{E}[\mathbf{z}_t\mathbf{u}_t'] = \mathbf{0}$ for estimated $\boldsymbol{\Gamma}$. Substitute the estimated components $\boldsymbol{\Gamma}\mathbf{z}_t$ and $\mathbf{u}_t$ for $\mathbf{w}_t$ in the GUM, leading to:

$$y_t = \boldsymbol{\beta}'\mathbf{z}_t + \boldsymbol{\gamma}'(\boldsymbol{\Gamma}\mathbf{z}_t + \mathbf{u}_t) + v_t = (\boldsymbol{\beta}' + \boldsymbol{\gamma}'\boldsymbol{\Gamma})\mathbf{z}_t + \boldsymbol{\gamma}'\mathbf{u}_t + v_t.$$

When $\boldsymbol{\gamma} = \mathbf{0}$, the coefficient of $\mathbf{z}_t$ remains $\boldsymbol{\beta}$, and because $\mathbf{z}_t$ and $\mathbf{u}_t$ are now orthogonal by construction, the estimate of $\boldsymbol{\beta}$ is unaffected by whether or not any or all $\mathbf{u}_t$ are included during selection.

To favour the incumbent theory, selection over additional variables can be undertaken at a stringent significance level to minimize the chances of spuriously selecting irrelevant variables. We suggest $\alpha = \min(0.001, 1/N)$. However, the approach protects against missing important explanatory variables, one such example of which is location shifts. The critical value for 0.1% in a Normal distribution is $c_{0.001} = 3.35$, so substantive regressors or shifts should still be easily retained. As noted in Castle et al. (2011), using IIS allows near Normality to be a reasonable approximation. However, a reduction from an integrated to a non-integrated representation requires non-Normal critical values, another reason for using tight significance levels during model selection. In practice, unless the parameters of the theory model have strong grounds for being of special interest, the orthogonalization step is unnecessary since the same outcome will be found just by retaining the theory variables when selecting over the additional candidates. An example of retaining a 'permanent income hypothesis' based consumption function relating the log of aggregate consumers' expenditure, c, to logs of income, i, and lagged c, orthogonalized with respect to the variables in Davidson et al. (1978), denoted DHSY, is provided in Hendry (2018).

When should an investigator reject the theory specification? As there are M additional variables included in the combined approach (in addition to the n theory variables which are not selected over), on average αM will be significant by chance, so if $M = 100$ and $\alpha = 1\%$ (so $c_{0.01} = 2.6$), on average there will be one adventitiously significant selection. Thus, finding that one of the additional variables was 'significant' would not be surprising even when the theory model was correct and complete. Indeed, the probabilities that none, one and two of the additional variables are significant by chance are 0.37, 0.37 and 0.18, leaving a probability of 0.08 of more than two being retained. However, using $\alpha = 0.5\%$ ($c_{0.005} = 2.85$), these probabilities become 0.61, 0.30 and 0.08 with almost no probability of 3 or more being significant; and 0.90, 0.09 and <0.01 for $\alpha = 0.1\%$, in which case retaining 2 or more of the additional variables almost always implies an incomplete or incorrect theory model.

When the total number of theory variables and additional variables exceeds the number of observations in the data sample (so $M + n = N > T$), our approach can still be implemented by splitting the variables into feasible sub-blocks, estimating separate projections for each sub-block, and replacing these subsets by their residuals. The n theory variables are retained without selection at every stage, only selecting over the (putatively irrelevant) variables at a stringent significance level using a multi-path block search of the form implemented in the model selection algorithm *Autometrics* (see Doornik 2009; Doornik and Hendry 2018). When the initial theory model is incomplete or incorrect—a likely possibility for the inflation illustration here—but some of the additional variables are relevant to explaining the phenomenon of interest, then an improved empirical model should result.

6.4 Applying the Combined Approach to UK Inflation Data

> **Interpreting regression equations**
> The simplest model considered below relates two variables, the dependent variable y_t and the explanatory variable x_t, $t = 1, \ldots, T$:
> $$y_t = \beta_0 + \beta_1 x_t + u_t.$$
> To conduct inference on this model, we assume that the innovations $u_1, \ldots u_T$ are independent and Normally distributed with a zero mean and constant variance, $u_t \sim \mathsf{IN}\left[0, \sigma_u^2\right]$, and that the parameter space for the parameters of interest $(\beta_0, \beta_1, \sigma_u^2)$ is not restricted. These assumptions need to be checked for valid inference, which is done by tests for residual autocorrelation (F_{ar}), non-Normality (χ^2_{nd}), autoregressive conditional heteroskedasticity (ARCH: $\mathsf{F}_{\mathsf{arch}}$, see Engle 1982), heteroskedasticity ($\mathsf{F}_{\mathsf{Het}}$), and functional form ($\mathsf{F}_{\mathsf{RESET}}$). If the assumptions for valid inference are satisfied, then we can interpret β_1 as the effect of a one unit increase in x_t on y_t, or an elasticity if x and y are in logs.

We start from the simplest equation relating inflation (denoted $\Delta p_t = p_t - p_{t-1}$ so Δ signifies a difference) to broad money growth (i.e., Δm_t) where lower case letters denote logs, P is the UK price level and M is its broad money stock:

$$\Delta p_t = \beta_0 + \beta_1 \Delta m_t + e_t \tag{6.1}$$

The two time series for annual UK data over 1874–2012 are shown in Fig. 6.1(a) and their scatter plot with a fitted regression line and the deviations therefrom in Panel (b).

At first sight, the hypothesis seems to have support: the two series are positively related (from Panel (b)) and tend to move together over time (from Panel (a)), although much less so after 1980. However, that leaves open the question of why: is inflation responding to money growth, or is more (less) money needed because the price level has risen (fallen)?

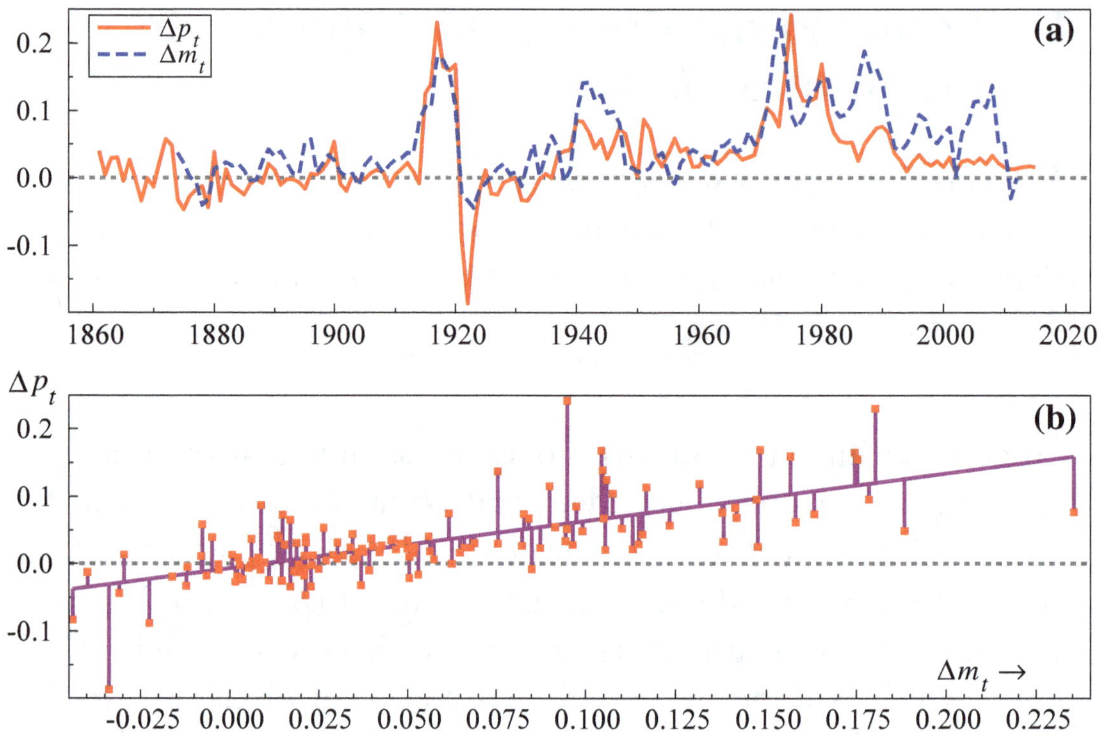

Fig. 6.1 (**a**) Time series of Δp_t and Δm_t; (**b**) scatter plot with the fitted regression of Δp_t on Δm_t and the deviations therefrom

The regression in (6.1) is estimated over 1877–2012 as:

$$\Delta p_t = \underset{(0.005)}{-\,0.005} + \underset{(0.063)}{0.69}\,\Delta m_t \tag{6.2}$$

$$\widehat{\sigma} = 4.1\% \;\; \mathsf{R}^2 = 0.47 \;\; \mathsf{F}_{\mathsf{ar}}(2, 132) = 30.7^{**} \;\; \mathsf{F}_{\mathsf{Het}}(2, 133) = 4.35^{*}$$
$$\chi^2_{\mathsf{nd}}(2) = 36.6^{**} \;\; \mathsf{F}_{\mathsf{arch}}(1, 134) = 8.94^{**} \;\; \mathsf{F}_{\mathsf{RESET}}(2, 132) = 1.27$$

The residual standard deviation, $\widehat{\sigma}$, is very large at 4%, with a 95% uncertainty range of 16%, when for the last 20 years, inflation has only varied between 1.5% and 3.5%.

Moreover, tests for residual autocorrelation (F_{ar}), non-Normality (χ^2_{nd}), autoregressive conditional heteroskedasticity (ARCH: $\mathsf{F}_{\mathsf{arch}}$) and heteroskedasticity ($\mathsf{F}_{\mathsf{Het}}$) all reject. Figure 6.2(a) records the fitted and actual values of Δp_t; (b) shows the residuals $\widehat{e}_t/\widehat{\sigma}$, (c) their density with a standard Normal for comparison; and (d) their residual correlogram.

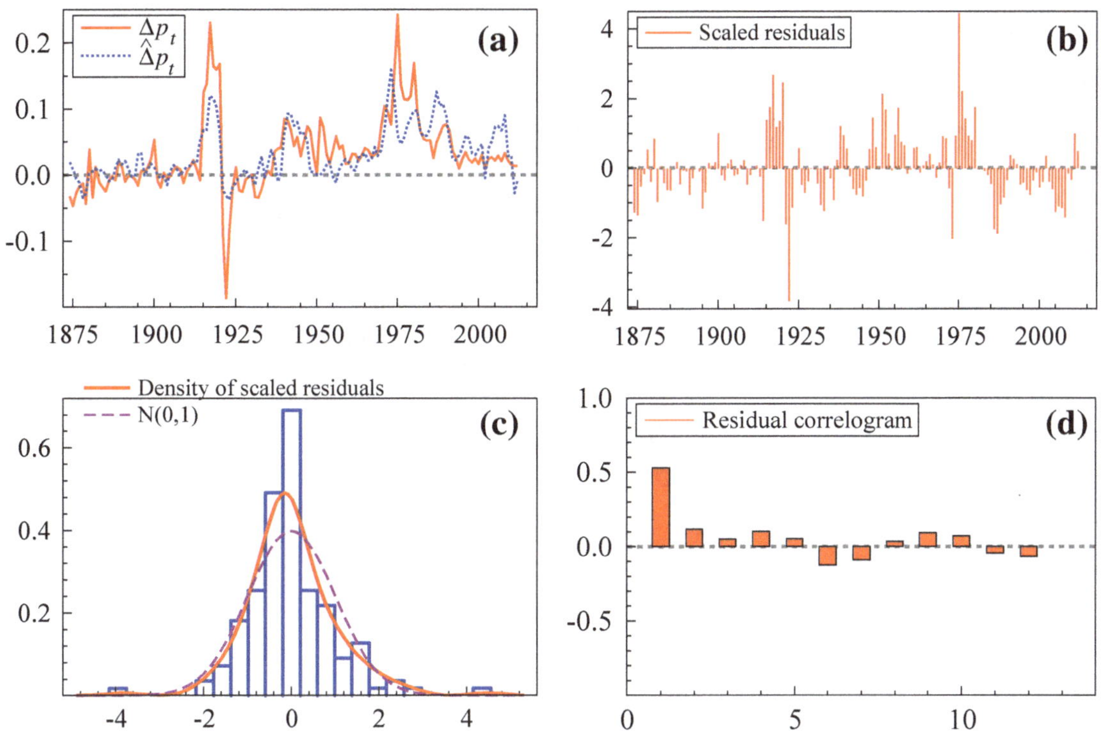

Fig. 6.2 (**a**) Fitted, $\widehat{\Delta p_t}$, and actual values, Δp_t, from (6.2); (**b**) scaled residuals $\widehat{e}_t/\widehat{\sigma}$; (**c**) their density with a standard Normal for comparison and (**d**) their residual correlogram

A glance at the test statistics in (6.2) and Fig. 6.2 shows that the equation is badly mis-specified, and indeed recursive estimation reveals considerable parameter non-constancy. The simplicity of the bivariate regression provides an opportunity to illustrate MIS, where both β_0 and β_1 are interacted with step indicators at every observation, so there are 271 candidate variables. Using $\alpha = 0.0001$ found 7 shifts in β_0 and 5 in β_1, halving $\widehat{\sigma}$ to 1.9%, and revealing a far from constant relationship between money growth and inflation.

Such a result should not come as a surprise given the large number of major regime changes impinging on the UK economy over the period as noted in Chapter 3, many relevant to the role of money. In particular, key financial innovations and changes in credit rationing included the introduction of personal cheques in the 1810s and the telegraph in the 1850s both reducing the need for multiple bank accounts just before our sample; credit cards in the 1950s; ATMs in the 1960s; deregulation of banks and building societies (the equivalent of US Savings and Loans) in the 1980s;

interest-bearing chequing accounts around 1984; and securitization of mortgages; etc.

First, to offer the incumbent theory a better chance, we added lagged values of Δp_{t-i} and Δm_{t-i} for $i = 1, 2$ to (6.2), but without indicators, which improves the fit to $\widehat{\sigma} = 3.3\%$ although three significant mis-specification tests remain as (6.3) shows.

$$\begin{aligned}\Delta p_t = &\underset{(0.09)}{0.67}\,\Delta p_{t-1} - \underset{(0.08)}{0.19}\,\Delta p_{t-2} + \underset{(0.10)}{0.40}\,\Delta m_t \\ &- \underset{(0.15)}{0.01}\,\Delta m_{t-1} - \underset{(0.11)}{0.02}\,\Delta m_{t-2} - \underset{(0.004)}{0.003}\end{aligned} \tag{6.3}$$

$$\widehat{\sigma} = 3.3\% \;\; \mathsf{R}^2 = 0.66 \;\; \mathsf{F}_{\mathsf{ar}}(1, 128) = 0.20 \;\; \mathsf{F}_{\mathsf{Het}}(10, 125) = 5.93^{**}$$

$$\chi^2_{\mathsf{nd}}(2) = 76.9^{**} \;\; \mathsf{F}_{\mathsf{arch}}(1, 134) = 7.73^{**} \;\; \mathsf{F}_{\mathsf{RESET}}(2, 128) = 0.13$$

Neither lag of money growth is relevant given the contemporaneous value, but both lags of inflation matter, suggesting about half of past inflation is carried forward, so there is a moderate level of persistence. Now applying IIS+SIS at $\alpha = 0.0025$ to (6.3) yielded $\widehat{\sigma} = 1.6\%$ with 4 impulse and 6 step indicators retained, but with all the coefficients of the economics variables being much closer to zero.

As the aim of this section is to illustrate our approach, and a substantive model of UK inflation over this period is available in Hendry (2015), we just consider four of the rival explanations that have been proposed. Thus to create a more general GUM for Δp_t, we also include the unemployment rate ($U_{r,t}$) relating to the original Phillips curve model of inflation (Phillips 1958); the potential output gap (measured by $(g_t - 0.019t)$ and adjusted to give a zero mean) and growth in GDP (Δg_t) to represent excess demand for goods and services (an even older idea dating back to Hume); wage inflation (Δw_t) as a cost push measure (a 1970s theme); and changes in long-term interest rates ($\Delta R_{L,t}$) reflecting the cost of capital. To avoid simultaneity, all variables are entered lagged one and two periods (including money growth) and the 2-period lag of the potential output gap is excluded to avoid multicollinearity between growth in GDP and the potential output gap, making $N = 14$ including the intercept before any indicators. The five additional variables are then orthogonalized with respect to Δm_t and lags of it and lags of Δp_t. To fully implement the strategy, lags of regressors should also be orthogonalized, but the resulting coefficients of the variables in common are close to those in the simpler model. Estimation delivers $\widehat{\sigma} = 3.3\%$ with an F-test on the additional variables of $\mathsf{F}(9, 121) = 2.66^{**}$, thereby rejecting the simple model, still with the three mis-specification tests significant.

Since the baseline theory model is untenable, its coefficients are not of interest, so we revert to the original measures of all the economic variables to facilitate interpretation of the final model. The economic variables are all retained while we select indicators by IIS and SIS at $\alpha = 0.0025$, choosing that significance level so that only a few highly significant indicators would be retained, with almost none likely to be significant by chance (with a theoretical retention rate of $271 \times 0.0025 = 0.68$ of an indicator). Nevertheless, five impulse and ten step indicators were selected, producing $\widehat{\sigma} = 1.2\%$ now with no mis-specification tests significant at 1%. Such a plethora of highly significant indicators implies that inflation is not being well explained even by the combination of all the theories. In fact the more general model in Hendry (2015) still needed 7 step indicators (though for somewhat different unexplained shifts) as well as dummies for the World Wars: sudden major shifts in UK inflation are not well explained by economic variables. We then selected over the 13 economic variables at the conventional significance level of 5%, forcing the intercept to be retained. Six were retained, with $\widehat{\sigma} = 1.2\%$ to deliver (only reporting the economic variables):

$$\begin{aligned}
\Delta p_t = \underset{(0.04)}{0.17}\,\Delta m_{t-2} - \underset{(0.10)}{0.46}\,U_{r,t-1} + \underset{(0.09)}{0.43}\,U_{r,t-2} - \underset{(0.03)}{0.10}\,gap_{t-1} \\
+ \underset{(0.03)}{0.23}\,\Delta w_{t-1} + \underset{(0.24)}{0.54}\,\Delta R_{L,t-1} + \underset{(0.01)}{0.02} \qquad (6.4)
\end{aligned}$$

$$\begin{aligned}
\widehat{\sigma} = 1.2\% \quad (\mathsf{R}^*)^2 = 0.96 \quad \mathsf{F}_{\mathsf{ar}}(2, 112) = 0.14 \\
\mathsf{F}_{\mathsf{Het}}(22, 108) = 1.97^* \\
\chi^2_{\mathsf{nd}}(2) = 1.63 \quad \mathsf{F}_{\mathsf{arch}}(1, 134) = 0.15 \\
\mathsf{F}_{\mathsf{RESET}}(2, 112) = 4.25^*
\end{aligned}$$

In contrast to the simple monetary theory of inflation, the model retains aspects of all the theories posited above. Now there is no direct persistence from past inflation, but remember that the step indicators represent persistent location shifts, so the mean inflation rate persists at different levels. Interesting aspects are how many shifts were found and that these location shifts seem to come from outside economics. The dates selected are consistent with that: 1914, 1920 and 1922, 1936 and 1948, 1950 and 1952, 1969, 1973 and 1980, all have plausible events, although they were not the only large unanticipated shocks over the last 150 years (e.g., the general strike). There is a much bigger impact from past wage growth than money growth as proximate determinants, but we have not modelled those to determine 'final' causes of what drives the shifts and evolution. Finally, the − then + coefficients on unemployment suggest it is changes therein rather than the levels that affect inflation.

The long-run relation after solving out the dynamics is:

$$\Delta p = \underset{(0.03)}{0.23}\,\Delta w + \underset{(0.04)}{0.17}\,\Delta m - \underset{(0.07)}{0.03}\,U_r - \underset{(0.03)}{0.10}\,gap + \underset{(0.24)}{0.54}\,\Delta R_L \tag{6.5}$$

The first two signs and magnitudes are easily interpreted as higher wage growth and faster money growth raise inflation. The negative unemployment coefficient is insignificant, consistent with its role probably being through changes. The hard to interpret output gap could be reflecting omitted variables and changes in the cost of capital raising inflation.

It is easy to think of other variables that could have an impact on the UK inflation rate, including the mark-up over costs used by companies to price their output; changes in commodity prices, especially oil; imported inflation from changes in world prices; changes in the nominal exchange rate; and changes in the National Debt among others, several of which are significant in the inflation model in Hendry (2015). Moreover, there is no strong reason to expect a constant relation between any of the putative explanatory variables and inflation given the numerous regime shifts that have occurred, the changing nature of money, and increasing globalization. In principle, MIS could be used where shifts are most likely, but in practice might be hard to implement at a reasonable significance level.

In our proposed combined theory-driven and data-driven approach, when the theory is complete it is almost costless in statistical terms to check the relevance of large numbers of other candidate variables, yet there is a good chance of discovering a better empirical model when the theory is incomplete or incorrect. Automatic model selection algorithms that allow retention of theory variables while selecting over many orthogonalized candidate variables can therefore deliver high power for the most likely explanatory variables while controlling spurious significance at a low level. Oh for having had the current technology in the 1970s! This is only partly anachronistic, as the theory in Hendry and Johansen (2015) could easily have been formulated 50 years ago. Combining the theory and data based approaches improves the chances of discovering an empirically well-specified, theory-interpretable model.

References

Castle, J. L., Doornik, J. A., and Hendry, D. F. (2011). Evaluating automatic model selection. *Journal of Time Series Econometrics*, **3(1)**. https://doi.org/10.2202/1941-1928.1097.

Castle, J. L., and Hendry, D. F. (2014). Semi-automatic non-linear model selection. In Haldrup, N., Meitz, M., and Saikkonen, P. (eds.), *Essays in Nonlinear Time Series Econometrics*, pp. 163–197. Oxford: Oxford University Press.

Davidson, J. E. H., Hendry, D. F., Srba, F., and Yeo, J. S. (1978). Econometric modelling of the aggregate time-series relationship between consumers' expenditure and income in the United Kingdom. *Economic Journal*, **88**, 661–692.

Doornik, J. A. (2009). Autometrics. In Castle, J. L., and Shephard, N. (eds.), *The Methodology and Practice of Econometrics*, pp. 88–121. Oxford: Oxford University Press.

Doornik, J. A., and Hendry, D. F. (2015). Statistical model selection with big data. *Cogent Economics and Finance*. http://www.tandfonline.com/doi/full/10.1080/23322039.2015.1045216#.VYE5bUYsAsQ.

Doornik, J. A., and Hendry, D. F. (2018). *Empirical Econometric Modelling Using PcGive: Volume I*, 8th Edition. London: Timberlake Consultants Press.

Engle, R. F. (1982). Autoregressive conditional heteroscedasticity, with estimates of the variance of United Kingdom inflation. *Econometrica*, **50**, 987–1007.

Hendry, D. F. (2015). *Introductory Macro-econometrics: A New Approach*. London: Timberlake Consultants. http://www.timberlake.co.uk/macroeconometrics.html.

Hendry, D. F. (2018). Deciding between alternative approaches in macroeconomics. *International Journal of Forecasting*, **34**, 119–135, with

'Response to the Discussants', 142–146. http://authors.elsevier.com/sd/article/S0169207017300997.

Hendry, D. F., and Doornik, J. A. (2014). *Empirical Model Discovery and Theory Evaluation.* Cambridge, MA: MIT Press.

Hendry, D. F., and Johansen, S. (2015). Model discovery and Trygve Haavelmo's legacy. *Econometric Theory,* **31**, 93–114.

Hendry, D. F., and Pretis, F. (2016). *All Change! The Implications of Non-stationarity for Empirical Modelling, Forecasting and Policy.* Oxford University: Oxford Martin School Policy Paper. http://www.oxfordmartin.ox.ac.uk/publications/view/2318.

Leamer, E. E. (1983). Let's take the con out of econometrics. *American Economic Review,* **73**, 31–43. Reprinted in Granger, C. W. J. (ed.) (1990), *Modelling Economic Series.* Oxford: Clarendon Press.

Phillips, A. W. H. (1958). The relation between unemployment and the rate of change of money wage rates in the United Kingdom, 1861–1957. *Economica,* **25**, 283–299. Reprinted as pp. 243–260 in R. Leeson (ed.) (2000) *A. W. H. Phillips: Collected Works in Contemporary Perspective.* Cambridge: Cambridge University Press.

7

Seeing into the Future

Abstract While empirical modelling is primarily concerned with understanding the interactions between variables to recover the underlying 'truth', the aim of forecasts is to generate useful predictions about the future regardless of the model. We explain why models must be different in non-stationary processes from those that are optimal' under stationarity, and develop forecasting devices that avoid systematic failure after location shifts.

Keywords Forecasting · Forecast failure · Forecast uncertainty · Hedgehog forecasts · Outliers · Location shifts · Differencing · Robust devices

In a stationary world, many famous theorems about how to forecast optimally can be rigorously proved (summarised in Clements and Hendry 1998):

1. causal models will outperform non-causal (i.e., models without any relevant variables);
2. the conditional expectation of the future value delivers the minimum mean-square forecast error (MSFE);

J. L. Castle and D. F. Hendry, *Modelling our Changing World*,
Palgrave Texts in Econometrics, https://doi.org/10.1007/978-3-030-21432-6_7

3. mis-specified models have higher forecast-error variances than correctly specified ones;
4. long-run interval forecasts are bounded above by the unconditional variance of the process;
5. neither parameter estimation uncertainty nor high correlations between variables greatly increase forecast-error variances.

Unfortunately, when the process to be forecast suffers from location shifts and stochastic trends, and the forecasting model is mis-specified, then:

1. non-causal models can outperform correct in-sample causal relationships;
2. conditional expectations of future values can be badly biased if later outcomes are drawn from different distributions (see Fig. 4.5);
3. the correct in-sample model need not outperform in forecasting, and can be worse than the average of several devices;
4. long-run interval forecasts are unbounded;
5. parameter estimation uncertainty can substantively increase interval forecasts; as can
6. changes in correlations between variables at or near the forecast origin.

The problem for empirical econometrics is not a plethora of excellent forecasting models from which to choose, but to find any relationships that survive long enough to be useful: as we have emphasized, the stationarity assumption must be jettisoned for observable variables in economics. Location shifts and stochastic trend non-stationarities can have pernicious impacts on forecast accuracy and its measurement: Castle et al. (2019) provide a general introduction.

7.1 Forecasting Ignoring Outliers and Location Shifts

To illustrate the issues, we return to the two data sets in Chapter 5 which were perturbed by an outlier and a location shift respectively, then modelled by IIS and SIS. The next two figures use the indicators found in those examples. In Fig. 7.1, the 1-step forecasts with and without the indicator show the former to be slightly closer to the outcome, and with a smaller interval forecast.

Both features seem sensible: an outlier is a transient perturbation, and providing it is not too large, its impact on forecasts should also be transient and not too great. The increase in the interval forecast is due to the rise in the estimated residual standard error from the outlier. Nevertheless, failing to model outliers can be very detrimental as Hendry and Mizon (2011) show when modelling an extension of the US food expenditure data noted above, which was of course, the origin of IIS finding the very large outliers in the 1930s, discussed in Sect. 5.1 as a robust estimation method.

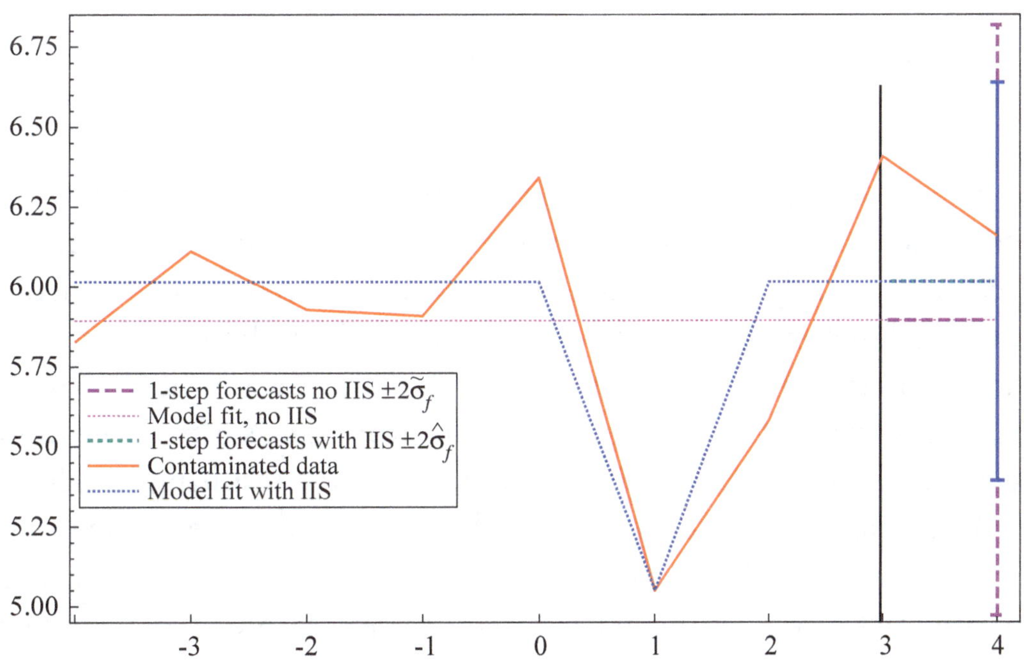

Fig. 7.1 1-step forecasts with and without the impulse indicator to model an outlier

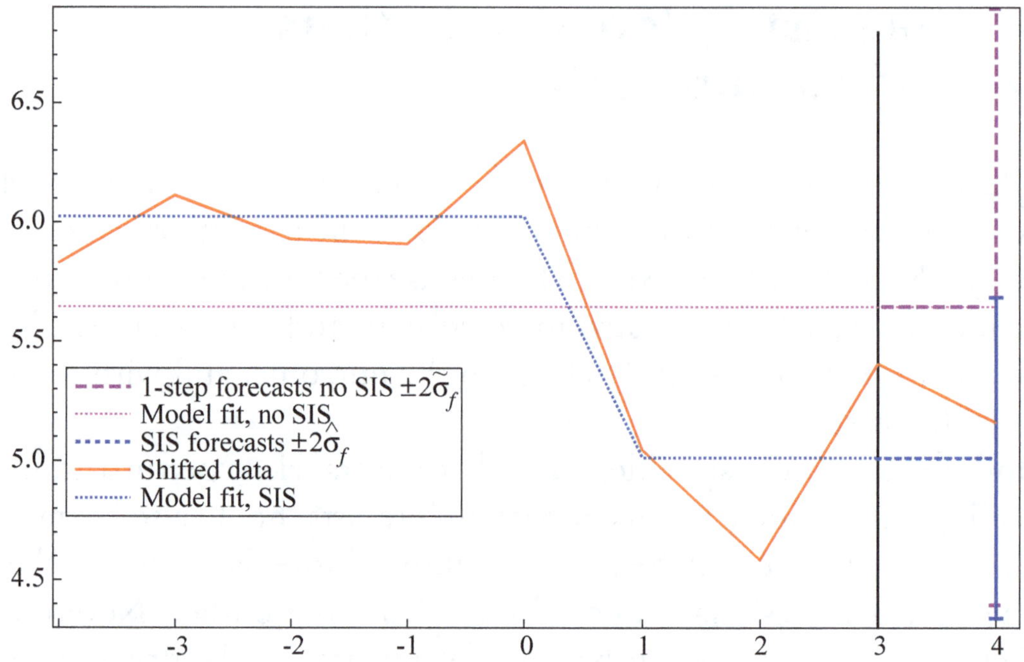

Fig. 7.2 1-step forecasts with and without the step indicator

However, the effect of omitting a step indicator that matches a location shift is far more serious as Fig. 7.2 shows. The 1-step forecast with the indicator is much closer to the outcome, with an even smaller interval forecast than that from the model without. Moreover, the forecast without the step indicator is close to the top of the interval forecast from the model with.

In Fig. 7.2, we (the writers of this book) know that the model with SIS matches the DGP (albeit with estimated rather than known parameters), whereas the model that ignores the location shift is mis-specified, and its interval forecast is hopelessly too wide—wider than the range of all previous observations. Castle et al. (2017) demonstrate the use of SIS in a forecasting context, where the step-indicator acts as a type of intercept correction when there has been a change in policy resulting in a location shift. An intercept correction changes the numerical value of the intercept in a forecasting model by adding a recent forecast error to put the forecast 'back on track'. SIS, along with other forms of robust device such as a conventional intercept correction, can greatly improve forecasts when they are subject to shifts at or near the forecast origin: see Clements and Hendry (1996).

7.2 Impacts of Stochastic Trends on Forecast Uncertainty

Because I(1) processes cumulate shocks, even using the correct in-sample model leads to much higher forecast uncertainty than would be anticipated on I(0) data. This is exemplified in Fig. 7.3 showing multi-period forecasts of log(GDP) starting in 1990 till 2030: the outcomes to 2016 are shown, but not used in the forecasts. Constant-change, or difference stationary, forecasts (dotted) and deterministic trend forecasts (dashed) usually make closely similar central forecasts as can be seen here. But deterministic linear trends do not cumulate shocks, so irrespective of the data properties, and hence even when the data are actually I(1), their uncertainty is measured as if the data were stationary around the trend.

Although the data properties are the same for the two models in Fig. 7.3, their estimated forecast uncertainties differ dramatically (bars and bands respectively), increasingly so as the horizon grows, due to the linear trend model assuming stable changes over time. Thus, model

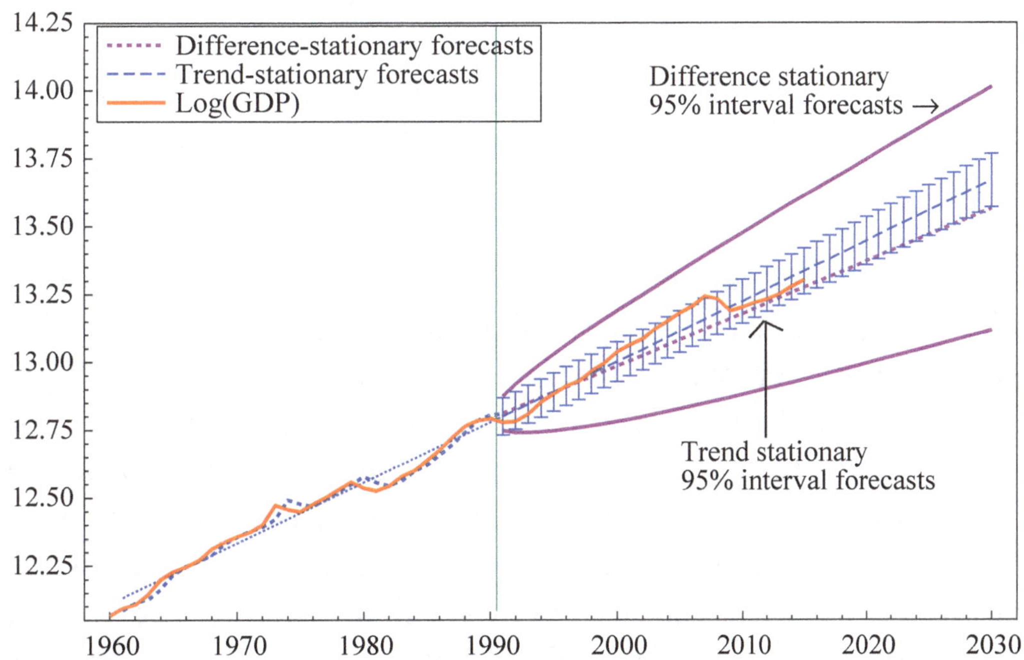

Fig. 7.3 Multi-period forecasts of log(GDP) using a non-stationary stochastic-trend model (dotted) and a trend-stationary model (dashed) with their associated 95% interval forecasts

choice has key implications for measuring forecast uncertainty, where misspecifications—such as incorrectly imposing linear trends—can lead to understating the actual uncertainty in forecasts. Although the assumption of a constant linear trend is rarely satisfactory, nevertheless, here almost all the outcomes between 1990 and 2016 lie within the bars. Conversely, the difference stationary interval forecasts are very wide. In fact, that model has considerable residual autocorrelation which the bands do not take into account, so over-estimate the uncertainty. However, caution is always advisable when forecasting integrated time series for long-periods into the future by either approach, especially from comparatively short samples.

7.3 Impacts of Location Shifts on Forecast Uncertainty

Almost irrespective of the forecasting device used, forecast failure would be rare in a stationary process, so episodes of forecast failure confirm that many time series are not stationary. Conversely, forecasting in the presence of location shifts can induce systematic forecast failure, unless the forecasting model accounts for the shifts.

Figure 7.4 shows some recent failures in 8-quarter ahead forecasts of US log real GDP. There are huge forecast errors (measured by the vertical distance between the forecast and the outcome), especially at the start of the 'Great Recession', which are not corrected till near the trough. We call these 'hedgehog' graphs since the successively over-optimistic forecasts lead to spikes like the spines of a hedgehog. It can be seen that the largest and most persistent forecast errors occur after the trend growth of GDP slows, or falls. This is symptomatic of a fundamental problem with many model formulations, which are equilibrium-correction mechanisms (EqCMs) discussed in Sect. 4.2: they are designed to converge back to the previous equilibrium or trajectory. Consequently, even when the equilibrium or trajectory shifts, EqCMs will persistently revert to the old equilibrium—as the forecasts in Fig. 7.4 reveal—until either the model is revised or the old equilibrium returns.

Figure 7.4 illustrates the difficulties facing forecasting deriving from wide-sense non-stationarity. However, the problem created by a location

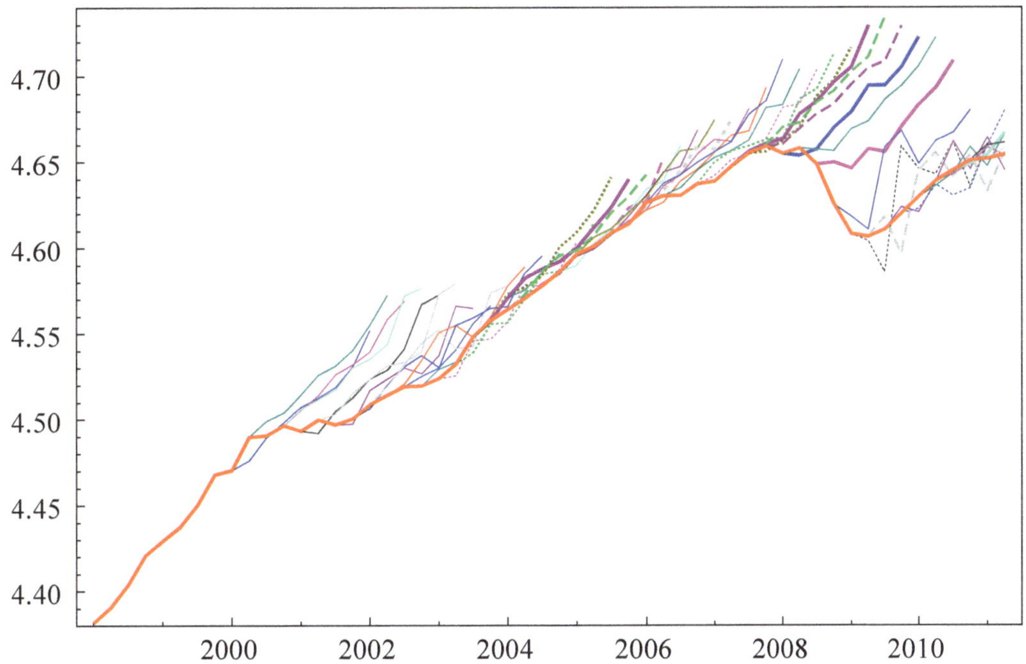

Fig. 7.4 US real GDP with many successive 8-quarter ahead forecasts

shift is not restricted to large forecast errors, but also affects the formation of expectations by economic actors: in theory models, today's expectation of tomorrow's outcome is often based on the 'most likely outcome', namely the conditional expectation of today's distribution of possible outcomes. In processes that are non-stationary from location shifts, previous expectations can be poor estimates of the next period's outcome. Figure 4.5 illustrated this problem, which has adverse implications for economic theories of expectations based on so-called 'rational' expectations. This issue also entails that many so-called structural econometric models constructed using mathematics based on inter-temporal maximization behavioural assumptions are bound to fail when the distributions involved shift as shown in Sect. 4.4.

7.4 Differencing Away Our Troubles

Differencing a break in a trend results in a location shift, as can be seen in Fig. 7.5, and in turn differencing a location shift produces an impulse, and a final differencing creates a 'blip'. All four types occur empirically.

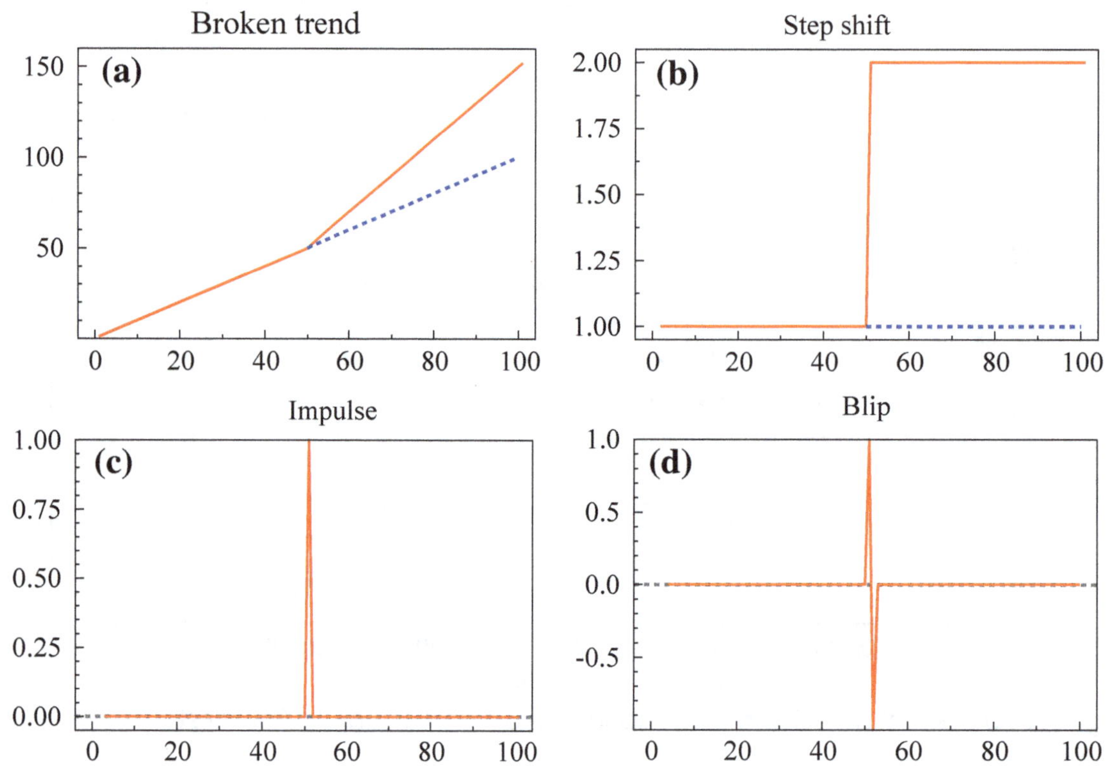

Fig. 7.5 Successively differencing a trend break in (**a**) creates a step shift in (**b**) an impulse in (**c**) and a 'blip' in (**d**)

Failing to allow for trend breaks or location shifts when forecasting entails extrapolating the wrong values and can lead to systematic forecast failure as shown by the dotted trajectories in Panels (a) and (b). However, failing to take account of an impulse or a blip just produces temporary errors, so forecasts revert back to an appropriate level rapidly. Consequently, many forecasts are reported for growth rates and often seem reasonably accurate: it is wise to cumulate such forecasts to see if the entailed levels are correctly predicted.

Figure 7.6 illustrates for artificial data: only a couple of the growth-rate outcomes lie above the 95% interval forecasts, but the levels forecasts are systematically downward biased from about observation 35. This is because the growth forecasts are on average slightly too low, which cumulates over time. The graphs show multi-step forecasts, but being simply a constant growth-rate forecast, the same interval forecasts apply at all steps ahead.

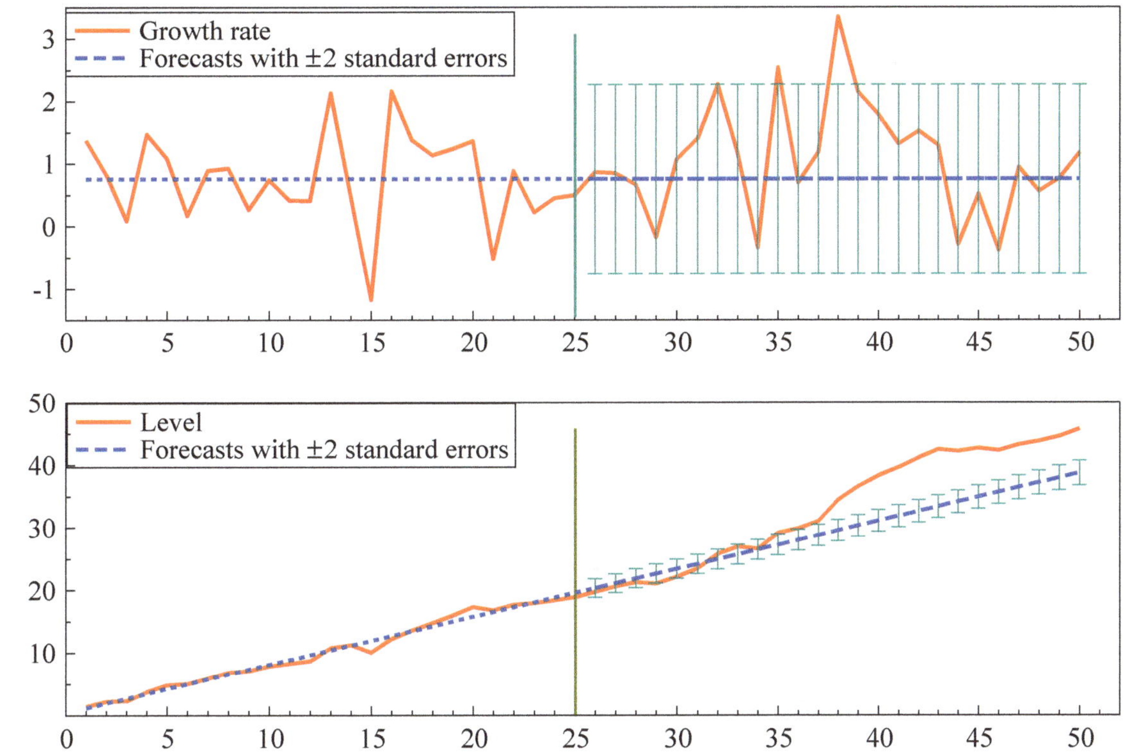

Fig. 7.6 Top panel: growth-rate forecasts; lower panel: implied forecasts of the levels

Constant growth-rate forecasts are of course excellent when growth rates stay at similar levels, but otherwise are too inflexible. An alternative is to forecast the next period's growth rate by the current value, which is highly flexible, but imposes a unit root even when the growth rate is I(0). Figure 7.3 contrasted deterministic trend forecasts with those from a stochastic trend, which had huge interval forecasts. Such intervals correctly reflect the ever increasing uncertainty arising from cumulating unrelated shocks when there is indeed a unit root in the DGP.

However, forecasting an I(0) process by a unit-root model also leads to calculating uncertainty estimates like those of a stochastic trend: the computer does not know the DGP, only the model it is fed. We must stress that interval forecasts are based on formulae that are calculated for the model used in forecasting. Most such formulae are derived under the assumption that the model is the DGP, so can be wildly wrong when that is not the case.

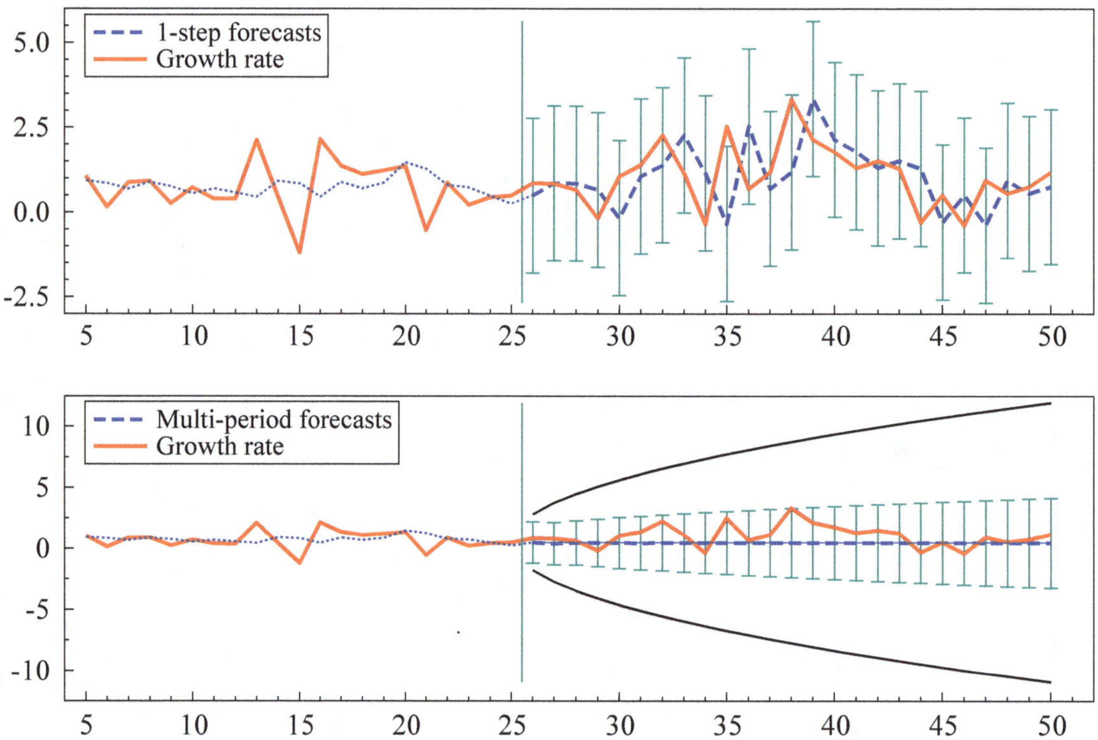

Fig. 7.7 Top panel: 1-step growth-rate forecasts from a 4-period moving average; lower panel: multi-period growth-rate forecasts with ± 2 standard errors from a random walk (bands) and a 4-period moving average of past growth rates (bars)

The top panel in Fig. 7.7 shows that 1-step growth-rate forecasts from a 4-period moving average of past growth rates with an imposed unit coefficient are much more flexible than the assumed constant growth rate, and only one outcome lies outside the 95% error bars. The two sets of multi-period interval forecasts in the lower panel of Fig. 7.7 respectively compare the growth rate and the 4-period moving average of past growth rates as their sole explanatory variables, both with an imposed unit coefficient to implement a stochastic trend. The average of the four most recent growth rates at the forecast origin, as against just one, produces a marked reduction in the interval forecasts despite still cumulating shocks.

A potential cost is that it will take longer to adjust to a shift in the growth rate. Here the growth rate is an I(0) variable, and it is the imposition of the unit coefficient that creates the increasing interval forecasts, but even so, the averaging illustrates the effects of smoothing. This idea of smoothing applies to the robust forecasting methods noted in the next section. Care is required in reporting interval forecasts for several steps ahead as their

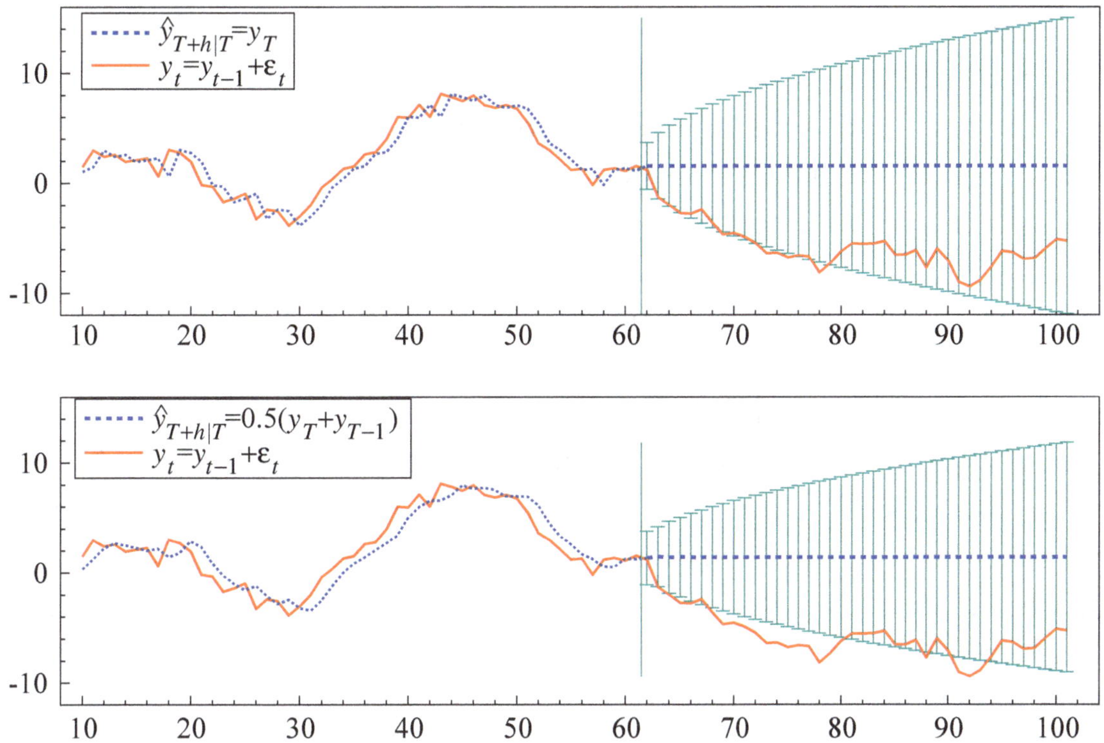

Fig. 7.8 Top panel: multi-period forecasts with ±2 standard errors from the DGP of a random walk; lower panel: multi-period forecasts from a 2-period moving average with ±2 calculated standard errors

calculation may reflect the properties of the model being used more than those of the DGP.

Conversely, trying to smooth a genuine random walk process by using a short moving average to forecast can lead to forecast failure as Fig. 7.8 illustrates. The DGP is the same in both panels, but the artificially smoothed forecasts in the lower panel have too small calculated interval forecasts.

7.5 Recommendations When Forecasting Facing Non-stationarity

Given the hazards of forecasting wide-sense non-stationary variables, what can be done? First, be wary of forecasting I(1) processes over long time horizons. Modellers and policy makers must establish when they are dealing with integrated series, and acknowledge that forecasts then entail increasing uncertainty. The danger is that uncertainty can be masked by using mis-specified models which can falsely reduce the reported uncertainty. An important case noted above is enforcing trend stationarity, as seen in Fig. 7.3, greatly reducing the measured uncertainty without reducing the actual, a recipe for poor policy and intermittent forecast failure. As Sir Alex Cairncross worried in the 1960s: 'A trend is a trend is a trend, but the question is, will it bend? Will it alter its course through some unforeseen force, and come to a premature end?' Alternatively, it is said that the trend is your friend till it doth bend.

Second, once forecast failure has been experienced, detection of location shifts (see Sect. 4.5) can be used to correct forecasts even with only a few observations, or alternatively it is possible to switch to more robust forecasting devices that adjust quickly to location shifts, removing much of any systematic forecast biases, but at the cost of wider interval forecasts (see e.g., Clements and Hendry 1999).

Nevertheless, we have also shown that one aspect of the explosion in interval forecasts from imposing an integrated model after a shift in an I(0) process (i.e., one that does not have a genuine unit root) is due to using just the forecast-origin value, and that can be reduced by using moving averages of recent values. In turbulent times, such devices are an example of a method with no necessary verisimilitude that can outperform the in-sample previously correct representation. Figure 7.9 illustrates the substantial improvement in the 1-step ahead forecasts of the log of UK GDP over 2008–2012 using a robust forecasting device compared to a 'conventional' method. The robust device has a much smaller bias and MSFE, but as it is knowingly mis-specified, clearly does not justify selecting it as an economic model—especially not for policy.

That last result implies that it is important to refrain from linking out-of-sample forecast performance of models to their 'quality' or verisimilitude. When unpredictable location shifts occur, there is no necessary link between forecast performance and how close the underlying model is to the truth. Both good and poor models can forecast well or badly depending on unanticipated shifts.

Third, the huge class of equilibrium-correction models includes almost all regression models for time series, autoregressive equations, vector autoregressive systems, cointegrated systems, dynamic-stochastic general

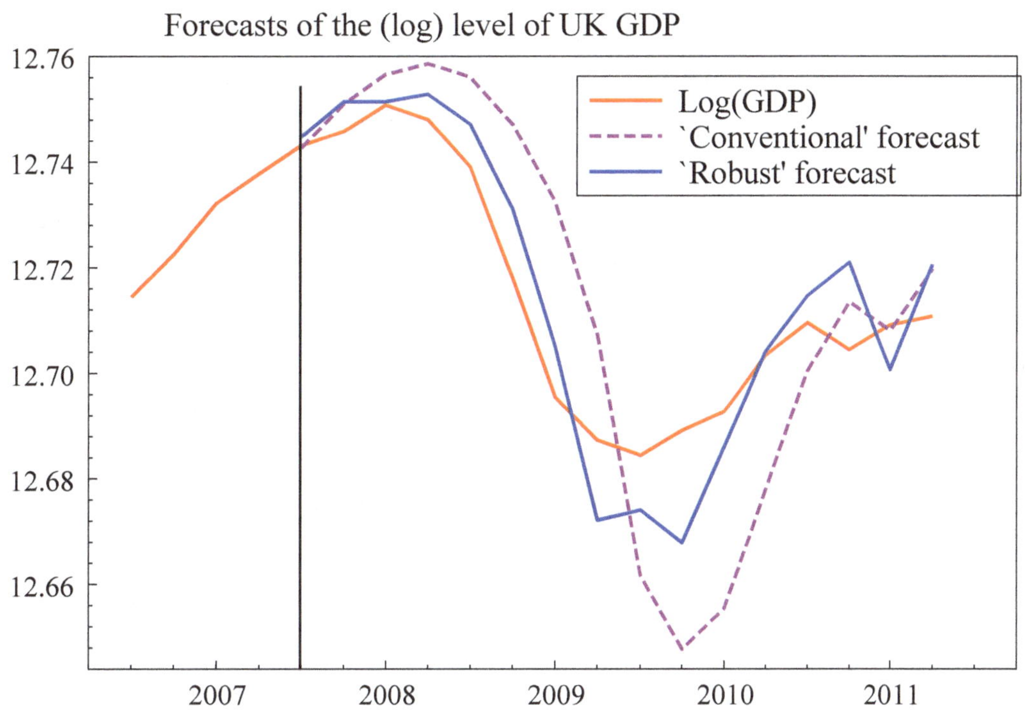

Fig. 7.9 1-step ahead forecasts of the log of UK GDP over 2008–2012 by 'conventional' and robust methods

equilibrium (DSGE) models, and many of the popular forms of model for autoregressive heteroskedasticity (see Engle 1982). Unfortunately, all of these formulations suffer from systematic forecast failure after shifts in their long-run, or equilibrium, means. Indeed, because they have in-built constant equilibria, their forecasts tend to go up (down) when outcomes go down (up), as they try to converge back to previous equilibria. Consequently, while cointegration captures equilibrium correction, care is required when using such models for genuine out-of-sample forecasts after any forecast failure has been experienced.

Fourth, Castle et al. (2018) have found that selecting a model for forecasting from a general specification that embeds the DGP does not usually entail notable costs compared to using the estimated DGP—an infeasible comparator with non-stationary observational data. Indeed when the exogenous variables need to be forecast, selection can even have smaller **MSFEs** than using a known DGP. That result matches an earlier finding in Castle et al. (2011) that a selected equation can have a smaller root mean square error (**RMSE**) for estimated parameters than those from estimating the DGP when the latter has several parameters that would not be significant on conventional criteria. Castle et al. (2018) suggest using looser than conventional nominal significance levels for in-sample selection, specifically 10% and 16% depending on the number of non-indicator candidate variables, and show that this choice is not greatly affected by whether or not location shifts occur either at, or just after, the forecast origin. The main difficulty is when an irrelevant variable that happens to be highly significant by chance has a location shift, which by definition will not affect the DGP but will shift the forecasts from the model, so forecast failure results. Here rapid updating after the failure will drive that errant coefficient towards zero in methods that minimize squared errors, so will be a transient problem.

Fifth, Castle et al. (2018) also conclude that some forecast combination can be a good strategy for reducing the riskiness of forecasts facing location shifts. Although no known method can protect against a shift after a forecast has been made, averaging forecasts from an econometric model, a robust device and a simple first-order autoregressive model frequently came near the minimum MSFE for a range of forecasting models on 1-step ahead forecasts in their simulation study. This result is consistent with many findings since the original analysis of pooling forecasts in Bates and Granger (1969), and probably reflects the benefits of 'portfolio diversification' known from finance theory. Clements (2017) provides a careful analysis of forecast combination. A caveat emphasized by Hendry and Doornik (2014) is that some pre-selection is useful before averaging to eliminate very bad forecasting devices. For example, the GUM is rarely a good device as it usually contains a number of what transpire to be irrelevant variables, and location shifts in these will lead to poor forecasts. Granger and Jeon (2004) proposed 'thick' modelling as a route to overcoming model uncertainty, where forecasts from all non-rejected specifications are combined. However, Castle (2017) showed that 'thick' modelling by itself neither avoids the problems of model mis-specification, nor handles forecast origin location shifts. Although 'thick' modelling is not formulated as a general-to-simple selection problem, it could be implemented by pooling across all congruent models selected by an approach like *Autometrics*.

References

Bates, J. M., and Granger, C. W. J. (1969). The combination of forecasts. *Operations Research Quarterly*, **20**, 451–468. Reprinted in T. C. Mills (ed.), *Economic Forecasting*. Edward Elgar, 1999.

Castle, J. L. (2017). Sir Clive W. J. Granger model selection. *European Journal of Pure and Applied Mathematics*, **10**, 133–156. https://ejpam.com/index.php/ejpam/article/view/2954.

Castle, J. L., Clements, M. P., and Hendry, D. F. (2019). *Forecasting: An Essential Introduction*. New Haven, CT: Yale University Press.

Castle, J. L., Doornik, J. A., and Hendry, D. F. (2011). Evaluating automatic model selection. *Journal of Time Series Econometrics*, **3(1)**. https://doi.org/10.2202/1941-1928.1097.

Castle, J. L., Doornik, J. A., and Hendry, D. F. (2018). Selecting a model for forecasting. Working paper, Economics Department, Oxford University.

Castle, J. L., Hendry, D. F., and Martinez, A. B. (2017). Evaluating forecasts, narratives and policy using a test of invariance *Econometrics*, **5(39)**. https://doi.org/10.3390/econometrics5030039.

Clements, M. P. (2017). Sir Clive W. J. Granger's Contributions to Forecasting. *European Journal of Pure and Applied Mathematics*, **10(1)**, 30–56. https://www.ejpam.com/index.php/ejpam/article/view/2949.

Clements, M. P., and Hendry, D. F. (1996). Intercept corrections and structural change. *Journal of Applied Econometrics*, **11**, 475–494.

Clements, M. P., and Hendry, D. F. (1998). *Forecasting Economic Time Series*. Cambridge: Cambridge University Press.

Clements, M. P., and Hendry, D. F. (1999). *Forecasting Non-stationary Economic Time Series*. Cambridge, MA: MIT Press.

Engle, R. F. (1982). Autoregressive conditional heteroscedasticity, with estimates of the variance of United Kingdom inflation. *Econometrica*, **50**, 987–1007.

Granger, C. W. J., and Jeon, Y. (2004). Thick modeling. *Economic Modelling*, **21**, 323–343.

Hendry, D. F., and Doornik, J. A. (2014). *Empirical Model Discovery and Theory Evaluation*. Cambridge, MA: MIT Press.

Hendry, D. F., and Mizon, G. E. (2011). Econometric modelling of time series with outlying observations. *Journal of Time Series Econometrics*, **3(1)**. https://doi.org/10.2202/1941-1928.1100.

8

Conclusions: The Ever-Changing Way Forward

Abstract In a world that is always changing, 'conclusion' seems an oxymoron. But we can summarize the story. First, that non-stationary data are pervasive in observational disciplines. Second, there are two main sources of non-stationarity deriving from evolutionary change leading to stochastic trends that cumulate past shocks and abrupt changes, especially location shifts, that lead to sudden shifts in distributions. Third, the resulting 'wide sense' non-stationarity not only radically alters empirical modelling approaches, it can have pernicious implications for inter-temporal theory, for forecasting and for policy. Fourth, methods for finding and neutralizing the impacts of distributional shifts from both sources are an essential part of the modeller's toolkit, and we proposed saturation estimation for modelling our changing world.

Keywords Theory formulations · Empirical modelling · Forecasting · Policy

J. L. Castle and D. F. Hendry, *Modelling our Changing World*,
Palgrave Texts in Econometrics, https://doi.org/10.1007/978-3-030-21432-6_8

Non-stationarity has important implications for inter-temporal theory, empirical modelling, forecasting and policy. Theory formulations need to account for humans inevitably facing disequilibria, so needing strategies for correcting errors after unanticipated location shifts. Empirical models must check for genuine long-run connections between variables using cointegration techniques, detect past location shifts, and incorporate feedbacks implementing how agents correct their previous mistakes. Forecasts must allow for the uncertainty arising from cumulating shocks, and could switch to robust devices after systematic failures. Tests have been formulated to check for models not being invariant to location shifts, and for policy changes even causing such shifts, potentially revealing that those models should not be used in future policy decisions.

Policy makers must recognise the challenges of implementing policy in non-stationary environments. Regulation of integrated processes, such as atmospheric CO_2 concentrations, is challenging due to their accumulation: for example, in climate policy, net-zero emissions are required to stabilise outcomes (see Allen 2015). Invariance of the parameters in policy models to a policy shift is a necessary condition for that policy to be effective and consistent with anticipated outcomes. The possibility of location shifts does not seem to have been included in risk models of financial institutions, even though such shifts will generate many apparently extremely unlikely successive bad draws relative to the prevailing distribution, as seen in Fig. 4.5.

Caution is advisable when acting on forecasts of integrated series or during turbulent times, potentially leading to high forecast uncertainty and systematic forecast failure, as seen in Figs. 7.8 and 7.9. Conversely, as noted in Sect. 3.2, the tools described above for handling shifts in time series enabled Statistics Norway to quickly revise their economic forecasts after Lehmann Brothers' bankruptcy. Demographic projections not only face evolving birth and death rates as in Fig. 2.3, but also sudden shifts, as happens with migration, so like economics, must tackle both forms of non-stationarity simultaneously.

Location shifts that affect the equilibrium means of cointegrating models initially cause systematic forecast failure, then often lead to incorrectly predicting rapid recovery following a fall, but later under-estimating a subsequent recovery. Using robust forecasting devices like those recorded in Fig. 7.9 after a shift or forecast failure can help alleviate both problems.

While this book has mainly considered time series data, similar principles apply to cross section and panel observational data. Panel data poses an additional problem of dependence. Time series data has the advantage of historical ordering, enabling sequential factorization to remove temporal dependence. Panel data requires a suitable exogenous ordering to apply sequential factorization which may not be obvious to the modeller. Methods to detect and model outliers and structural breaks may be particularly important in panel data, where individual heterogeneity accounts for much of the data variability. See Pretis et al. (2018) for an example of IIS applied to a fixed-effects panel model looking at the impacts of climate change on economic growth. IIS is equivalent to allowing for a 'fixed effect' for every observation in the panel, and accounting for these country-year individual effects proved invaluable in isolating the effects of climate variation on economic growth.

References

Allen, M. (2015). Short-lived promise? The science and policy of cumulative and short-lived climate pollutants. Oxford Martin policy paper, Oxford Martin School, Oxford, UK. https://www.oxfordmartin.ox.ac.uk/downloads/briefings/PolicyNote-SLCPs.pdf.

Pretis, F., Schwarz, M., Tang, K., Haustein, K., and Allen, M. R. (2018). Uncertain impacts on economic growth when stabilizing global temperatures at 1.5°C or 2°C warming. *Philosophical Transactions of the Royal Society*, **A376**, 20160460. https://doi.org/10.1098/rsta.2016.0460.

Author Index

J. L. Castle and D. F. Hendry, *Modelling our Changing World*,
Palgrave Texts in Econometrics, https://doi.org/10.1007/978-3-030-21432-6

Subject Index

J. L. Castle and D. F. Hendry, *Modelling our Changing World*,
Palgrave Texts in Econometrics, https://doi.org/10.1007/978-3-030-21432-6